Writing from Within 2
Second Edition

TEACHER'S MANUAL

Arlen Gargagliano
& Curtis Kelly

CAMBRIDGE UNIVERSITY PRESS
Cambridge, New York, Melbourne, Madrid, Cape Town,
Singapore, São Paulo, Delhi, Mexico City

Cambridge University Press
The Edinburgh Building, Cambridge CB2 8RU, UK

Published in the United States of America by Cambridge University Press, New York

www.cambridge.org
Information on this title: www.cambridge.org/9780521188333

© Cambridge University Press 2012

This publication is in copyright. Subject to statutory exception
and to the provisions of relevant collective licensing agreements,
no reproduction of any part may take place without the written
permission of Cambridge University Press.

First published 2012

A catalogue record for this publication is available from the British Library

ISBN 978-0-521-18834-0 Student's Book
ISBN 978-0-521-18833-3 Teacher's Manual

ISBN 978-0-521-18833-3 Paperback

Cambridge University Press has no responsibility for the persistence or
accuracy of URLs for external or third-party internet websites referred to in
this publication, and does not guarantee that any content on such websites is,
or will remain, accurate or appropriate. Information regarding prices, travel
timetables, and other factual information given in this work is correct at
the time of first printing but Cambridge University Press does not guarantee
the accuracy of such information thereafter.

Contents

Plan of the book iv

Introduction vi

Guidelines for using Writing vii
from Within 2

1 About me 1

2 Career consultant 7

3 A dream come true 12

4 Invent 17

5 It changed my life! 22

6 Exciting destinations 27

7 Classifying classmates 32

8 The job interview 37

9 Personal goals 42

10 Architect 47

11 My role models 52

12 Be a reporter 57

Plan of the book

	Writing assignment
Unit 1 *About me*	■ One paragraph about things you like to do
Unit 2 *Career consultant*	■ A composition about an appropriate career for your partner
Unit 3 *A dream come true*	■ A magazine article about your partner's future success
Unit 4 *Invent*	■ A composition about an invention
Unit 5 *It changed my life!*	■ A composition about an important event in your life
Unit 6 *Exciting destinations*	■ A guidebook article
Unit 7 *Classifying classmates*	■ A research report about your classmates
Unit 8 *The job interview*	■ An article about good and bad interview techniques
Unit 9 *Personal goals*	■ A letter to yourself about your goals
Unit 10 *Architect*	■ A composition about your own dorm design
Unit 11 *My role models*	■ A composition about an important person in your life
Unit 12 *Be a reporter*	■ A newspaper article

Organizational focus	Editing focus	Just for fun assignment
- Expository paragraphs - Topic sentences	- Paragraph format	- Writing a paragraph about yourself
- Supporting logical conclusions	- Using conjunctions *and*, *but*, and *so*	- Writing an e-mail requesting information
- Supporting topic sentences with facts and examples	- Direct and indirect speech	- Making a résumé
- Definition paragraphs - Attention getters	- Avoiding repetition	- Writing an e-mail to a company about a product
- Cause-and-effect paragraphs - Introductory paragraphs	- Cause-and-effect words	- Designing a greeting card
- Suggestions - Process paragraphs	- Using modifiers	- Making a list of travel tips
- Classification paragraphs - Concluding paragraphs	- Using commas	- Making a presentation on your research
- Comparison-contrast paragraphs	- Giving advice	- Reporting an interview results
- Persuasive paragraphs	- Parallel construction	- Writing positive things about classmates
- Division paragraphs	- Articles	- Making a poster advertising a dorm
- Development-by-example compositions - Linking paragraphs	- Subject-verb agreement	- Writing a letter to someone who has influenced you
- Using objective, persuasive, and entertaining styles - Newspaper headlines and styles	- Verb variety	- Designing a class newspaper

Introduction

We, the authors of *Writing from Within 2*, believe that the greatest hurdle our student writers face is learning how to organize their writing. Therefore, the main focus of this text is teaching students how to generate topics, write cohesive paragraphs, and organize them into clear, logical expository compositions. We focus on expository writing – or explaining – because it uses an organizational style that differs from the styles used in other languages, and also because it represents the kind of writing our learners will have to do in academic or business environments.

We also believe that excellence in student writing goes beyond mere accuracy or the ability to mimic models. Excellence comes from writing that leads to discovery of self, of ideas, and of others; self-expression is its own reward. We believe students should be *pulled* into learning through interesting and expressive activities rather than *pushed* into learning through fear of failure. Therefore, we have chosen to offer writing topics that will challenge your learners' creativity, lead them to introspection, and, most importantly, allow them to experience writing as a joyful process.

The focus of each unit is a writing assignment. Some are introspective: For example, learners are asked to reflect on a major life event that has led to growth. Others are more conventional but task-based: Learners are asked to plan a tour of a city and to publish a class newspaper. In this way, humanistic writing assignments are balanced with task-based writing assignments to provide a broad range of writing experiences. In addition, each unit ends with an optional expansion activity that gives learners the opportunity to apply their new skills to a different task.

Every unit offers learners different organizational tools, which are practiced in prewriting exercises. Learners analyze the organization in paragraphs using different expository modes, such as division, classification, or cause and effect, and do exercises on writing attention getters, identifying good topic sentences, using different styles, and so on. At the center of each unit (with the exception of Unit 1) is a composition assignment. Editing skills are taught by giving learners practice in mechanics and grammar. Each unit takes three to five hours of class time to complete, and although the syllabus is developmental, it is not necessary to do each unit in order.

The Teacher's Manual is designed to give specific ideas on using the Student's Book and tips for adapting it to suit your classroom. We suggest you take the time to familiarize yourself with the style and themes of the Student's Book before you begin teaching.

Writing is a skill. We tell our students that learning to write is like learning to play a musical instrument: The more they practice, the better they will be. *Writing from Within 2* is designed to demonstrate to learners that they have the knowledge and ability within to develop this skill. We hope they will enjoy this text, and we look forward to hearing your comments.

Arlen Gargagliano
Curtis Kelly

Guidelines for using *Writing from Within 2*

How should I use the Teacher's Manual?

Each unit in the Teacher's Manual is about five pages long. It is divided into four sections: (1) a short **Overview** that tells you what the students will do and learn, (2) a list of **Key points** – things to keep in mind, and (3) detailed **Instructions** for each lesson. Experienced teachers need only read the first two sections.

What is the basic organization of a unit in the Student's Book?

The book uses a process approach. At the center of each unit is a composition assignment. Each one-page lesson is a prewriting, writing, or postwriting activity. More than half are prewriting.

Prewriting

Part 1: Brainstorming   The topic is introduced and writing ideas are generated.

Part 2: Analyzing a paragraph   Students analyze the organization used in a model paragraph.

Parts 3–5: Learning about organization, Working on content   Students gather information for their composition and learn expository organizational skills.

Part 6: Analyzing a model   Students analyze a model composition just like the one they must write.

Writing

Part 7: Write!   Students receive instructions for writing the composition.

Postwriting

Part 8: Editing   Students correct grammatical errors common to beginning writers and edit their compositions.

Part 9: Giving feedback   Students exchange compositions with other students for review and feedback.

Just for fun   Students might do an optional writing activity that helps them augment their newly gained skills.

How is Unit 1 different?

In other units, students are assigned a multiparagraph composition, but in Unit 1, just a single expository paragraph is included. The focus is on topic sentences and paragraph writing.

Why should students write topic sentences and underline them?

Interestingly, according to research, only a quarter of all published paragraphs actually contain topic sentences. Topic sentences are, nonetheless, a powerful teaching tool. In order to write a topic sentence, the student must know what the main idea of the paragraph is, which research shows exists in all paragraphs. By asking students to underline their topic sentences, teachers can evaluate the coherence and cohesion of the paragraph and identify the intended organization of a composition at a glance. We recommend that you use this technique.

What are some ways this book teaches organization?

First, in addition to learning what a paragraph is and what a topic sentence is, students are given practice in using transition words. Transition words provide the framework by which the rest of a paragraph is organized: Transition words such as *first*, *second*, or *third* are used to introduce a series of subtopics. *For example* or *in one case* are used to add details. *However* or *on the other hand* are used to show a differing idea or subtopic. *In conclusion* or *therefore* are used to show an inference or summary. Transition words hold the ideas in a paragraph together and delineate their hierarchy.

Second, students are given practice using the different ways expository writing is organized. These expository writing modes include process, division, comparison and contrast, cause and effect, definition, example, and so on. The model paragraphs in *Analyzing a paragraph* introduce these different ways of organizing.

Third, students must learn to write good introductory paragraphs. Unlike some other languages, English tends to be top-heavy, with the main idea usually at the beginning and developed through subtopics after that.

Finally, students are given opportunities to practice using some of the other tools provided, such as outlining, writing a conclusion, linking sentences, and using paragraph transitions. These are presented throughout the text.

How is English organization different from that of other languages?

Descriptive and narrative writing use spatial and chronological organization, so these types of writing are similar in all languages. Expository and persuasive writing are not. The style of organization used for these types of writing is language-specific, and it is influenced by the different ways cultures value logic, intuition, and assertion. *Writing from Within 2* offers more expository than persuasive writing, because this is the most common type of writing used at school, at work, and on the Internet.

So what are some of the features of English expository organization? First, it is usually (but not always) top-oriented, with a main idea given at the beginning, and every following statement either adding to that idea or introducing another idea on the same level. Second, English is topically organized. Each paragraph has a single topic, and all its contents should be a part of that topic. Third, English expository writing tends toward logic and assertion. It tends to be less anecdotal, less intuitive, more linear, and more declarative than most other languages.

What part of the writing process should I focus on, and how should I correct my students' papers?

If teaching organization is your main goal, then spend more time on prewriting activities. If accuracy is your goal, then spend more time on revision and editing activities. We recommend that you set organization as your main goal, since research shows that this writing skill is so important. Many teachers tend to set accuracy as their goal and engage in extensive error correction, but other research suggests that correction is only effective when the corrections are made on the syntactic structures the learners are in the process of acquiring and when the learners have an opportunity to work with the corrections.

If you teach large classes, error correction might not even be an option, so we suggest you only correct organizational errors, such as poor topic sentences or introductory paragraphs. If you do correct errors, you may wish to devise a system whereby you correct only one kind of error in each composition, such as those related to the syntactic structure presented in the editing lesson. Even so, it is better to simply mark errors and have students make the corrections themselves.

What does the peer feedback activity (after the editing lesson) do?

Peer feedback is not the same as peer correction, and yet it achieves some of the same goals. Peer feedback gives the learners contact with models written by their peers and strengthens their ability to evaluate writing. When comments from peers on the strengths and weaknesses of a piece go back to the authors, the authors are getting feedback that sheds light directly on their ability to communicate and organize. Of even greater importance, though, is that peer feedback makes students feel that they are writing for a real audience, not just the teacher.

How can I deal with mixed levels of students in the same class?

Because the writing activities are open-ended and allow students to write at their level of competence, mixed levels should not be much of a problem. In some of the more closed-ended exercises, however, grouping students of the same level together might work better, or in some cases grouping students of different levels might work better. Whether you should mix or separate students of different levels depends on a number of factors, including learning styles, culture, and classroom dynamics. Experiment.

A greater problem might exist when some students finish an activity before the others and are left with nothing to do. Keep in mind that it is not necessary for every student to answer every question for learning to occur, and the "compare answers with a partner" option at the end of many exercises exists, in part, to help alleviate this problem.

Can I skip certain parts?

The *Key points* section of the Teacher's Manual indicates the minimum set of lessons, usually four, that must be completed in order to write the composition. Units can also be skipped or done in a different order. Just be sure that you teach your students how to write paragraphs with topic sentences before you start Unit 2, and introductory and concluding paragraphs before you go on to the second half of the book.

How often should I give homework?

This depends entirely on how your class is scheduled and the type of students you are teaching. Most of the activities can be done as homework.

How should I grade/assess students' writing?

The grading system you employ should reflect your teaching goals and the grading standards set by your school. A number of possibilities exist: In addition to grading aspects such as homework completion and attendance, you will probably evaluate compositions as well. You can grade all of the compositions and ask students to keep them in portfolios, or you can grade only some, having students write them in class as tests. You can assign grades by merely rating the organizational features, such as topic sentences, paragraphs, introductions, and overall content, or you can rate accuracy or rhetorical quality as well.

1 About me

Overview

As an introductory unit, the main writing assignment is a paragraph rather than a whole composition. The purpose of the unit is to familiarize students with the basic unit organization used throughout the text and the ten lessons that compose a unit, and to introduce some basic organization tools they will be using throughout the course. In regard to the latter, they learn how to separate general ideas from specific ideas, how to write topic sentences, and how to format paragraphs. Students will be given the opportunity to get to know one another better in the final optional lesson.

This unit introduces the basic structure of an expository paragraph. Students will learn how to organize a paragraph around one main idea and support it.

Key points

This unit is different from the other units. It is somewhat of a review unit on paragraph writing, as studied in *Writing from Within 1*. The unit is designed, however, so that use of *Writing from Within 1* is not a prerequisite.

Concentrate on getting your students to understand topic sentences. Although not all real paragraphs actually have them, they are a powerful teaching tool and will be used throughout the book.

If your students do not know one another, we suggest you do not skip the optional *Just for fun* activity. It will help to build student relationships.

Sections can be skipped. A minimal set of sections might include Parts 5, 6, and 7. You can also save time by assigning some sections as homework.

1 Brainstorming page 1

Brainstorming is a means of activating background knowledge on a subject and generating ideas for later writing. It is a free-association activity that lets students access all they know on a topic, write it down, and, to some degree, organize it. Allow students to experiment, but try to keep them from talking to one another during this activity.

- Draw a brain and a storm cloud on the board.
- Tell students that *to brainstorm* means "to write new ideas quickly."
- Read the information box *Brainstorming* at the top of page 1.
- Say: *Let's brainstorm together.* Write *New York* on the board. Ask: *What does New York make you think of?*
- Write a few words as examples on the board, such as *tall buildings*, *exciting*, and *great museums*. Then call on students to give you more words. Write them on the board.

1

- Read the instructions for Step 1 aloud.
- Write on the board: *Things I like to do: take pictures, sing, read.*
- Call on a student to read the *Things I like to do* list aloud.

2

- Read the instructions for Step 2 aloud and point out that this brainstorm takes one of Anna's ideas and breaks it down into smaller examples.
- Have students complete this step individually. Set a time limit of three to five minutes.
- Walk around the classroom. Encourage students and give them new vocabulary as necessary.

3

- Read the instructions for Step 3 aloud.
- Divide the class into pairs.
- Have students compare answers and add more information to their list.
- Call on some students to read their list of ideas aloud to the class or write ideas on the board.

> Later in this unit . . . Call on a student to read this aloud.

Unit 1 *About me* 1

2 Analyzing a paragraph page 2

The *Analyzing a paragraph* activities serve two purposes: They teach students some tools for basic organization, such as transition words, topic sentences, and so on; and they introduce the expository mode needed for that unit, such as development by example, definition, cause and effect, division, classification, and so on.

- This paragraph shows a basic expository style: taking a topic and breaking it down into subtopics, and then supporting each subtopic with examples and explanations.
- *Expository writing* means "writing that explains something," and is the main focus of this book.

1

- Write *Main idea* on the board. Tell students that in most paragraphs, each sentence is connected to the main idea.
- Have students read the paragraph individually.
- Call on students to read the paragraph aloud, sentence by sentence.
- Have students answer 1a–c individually. Walk around the classroom to encourage and help students.

> **Answers**
> 1. a. Things I don't like to do
>   b. The first sentence: There are many things that I don't like to do, but the most common ones are ironing, being in large crowds, and driving in the city.
>   c. ironing; it takes so much time
>   going to crowded places; I feel uncomfortable
>   driving in the city; it's difficult

2

- Divide the class into pairs and have students compare answers.
- Go over the answers as a class.
- Explain that this is an expository paragraph and that students will be writing paragraphs like this in the course. Explain that *expository writing* means "writing that explains what something is," and that it is the main type of writing used in school and business reports.

> **Talk about it.** Read this aloud and have students talk with their partners for about five minutes.

> ***Optional activity***
> **What's the main idea?**
> Give groups of students copies of paragraphs taken from their reading skills textbooks. Each paragraph should have a different main idea. Have students read the paragraphs to find the main ideas and discuss their answers with the group. Have students compare answers with a partner. Go over answers as a class.

3 Learning about organization page 3

The *Learning about organization* and *Learning more about organization* activities are just that. They introduce a set of tools used to organize English writing, especially expository writing. The sections include instructions on how to write topic sentences, how to write introductory paragraphs, how to use support, and so on.

- This section teaches students the relationship between general and specific information.
- Read the information box *Expository paragraphs* at the top of page 3.
- Explain what *general* and *specific* mean. Direct students' attention to the paragraph in Part 2 on the previous page, and point out how they identified the "specific parts" that support the general "main idea."
- On the board, write:

    General information   Specific information
    animals
    colors
    music

- Call on students to give you specific information, such as *horse*, *green*, and *classical music*, to complete the chart on the board.

1

- Read the instructions for Step 1 aloud.
- Have students read the examples in 1a–c.
- Explain vocabulary as needed.

2 Unit 1 *About me*

> *Optional activity*
>
> **Be more specific**
>
> Ask students to add additional specific information to the charts in Step 1.

2

- Read the instructions for Step 2 aloud.
- Have students complete 2a–c individually.
- Go over answers as a class.

> *Answers*
>
> 2. a. G: TV shows
>   b. G: ways to use the Internet
>   c. G: reasons to have a Facebook page

3

- Read the instructions for Step 3 aloud.
- Have students complete 3a–c individually.
- Walk around the classroom, helping students as necessary.

4

- Have students compare answers with a partner.
- Go over answers as a class.

> *Optional activity*
>
> **Generally speaking**
>
> Prepare several cards with one item of general information and three items of specific information. For example:
>
> | *General information* | *Specific information* |
> |---|---|
> | office machines | telephones |
> | | computers |
> | | fax machines |
>
> In groups, have students take turns choosing cards and reading the specific information. The student who guesses the general information first keeps the card. The student with the most cards at the end of the game is the winner.

4 Learning more about organization
page 4

- This section teaches students how to identify and write topic sentences.
- Write *Topic sentences* on the board.
- Read the information box *Topic sentences* at the top of page 4.
- Ask students to look back at the paragraph on page 2 and find the topic sentence.
- Elicit the answer: *There are many things that I don't like to do, but the most common ones are ironing, being in large crowds, and driving in the city.*

1

- Have students read the paragraph excerpts in Step 1.
- Have students mark the best topic sentences in 1a–i with a *T*.

2

- Divide the class into pairs.
- Have students compare answers with a partner.

3

- Read the instructions for Step 3 aloud. Explain the meanings of the words used to describe poor topic sentences.
- In pairs or individually, have students mark the other sentences in Step 1.
- Go over answers as a class.

> *Answers for 1 and 3*
>
> a. N
> b. P
> c. T
> d. C
> e. T
> f. G
> g. S
> h. T
> i. N

5 Working on content page 5

The *Working on content* and *Working more on content* activities are where students generate content for their compositions.

1

- Read the instructions and example at the top of page 5 aloud.
- Write another example on the board, such as:
  G games I enjoy watching
  S the Osaka Tigers
  S World Cup soccer
  S volleyball in the park
- Do not erase the board. You will use the list again in Step 2.
- Have students look at their brainstorming lists from page 1 and underline three items of general information. Have them write the general and specific information in 1a–c.
- Walk around the classroom, helping students as necessary.

2

- Read the instructions and example for Step 2 aloud.
- Ask a student to give you a topic sentence for the example you wrote in Step 1, such as, *There are some sports I enjoy watching.*
- Write the topic sentence the student gives you on the board.
- Have students complete Step 2 individually.
- Walk around and check students' books to be sure they understand. Help them if necessary.

3

- Read the instructions for Step 3 aloud.
- Have students circle the letter of the sentence they will use to write a paragraph in Part 7.

6 Analyzing a model page 6

The *Analyzing a model* activities give students a piece of writing, often written by other students, to model the kind of writing they will be asked to do in the following lesson: *Write!* Whereas some teachers worry that giving students models similar to their own writing leads to copying the model, this is not really a problem in *Writing from Within*, since the writing assignments are so personal. Lower-level students might imitate sentence forms and vocabulary, but we consider this a positive learning experience.

1

- Have individual students read the paragraph aloud, sentence by sentence.
- Have students complete 1a–c individually.

> **Answers**
> 1. a. places I like
>   b. Near my apartment, there are three places I like to go to.
>   c. the My Thai restaurant, Powell's Bookstore, the park

2

- Have students compare answers with a partner.
- Go over answers as a class.

7 Write! page 7

The *Write!* section is the heart of the unit: the composition writing assignment. The six preceding parts represent prewriting activities, where students learn the forms needed for this assignment and generate content for it. The two lessons following the post-writing activities allow students to polish or reflect on their and one another's writing.

1

- Read the instructions for Step 1 aloud.
- Have students complete 1a–b using the topic they chose on page 5.

2

- Read the instructions for Step 2 aloud.
- Have students write their own paragraph. Remind them to underline the topic sentence.
- Walk around the classroom, helping students as necessary.

3

- Read the instructions for Step 3 aloud.
- Ask students to check the boxes in the checklist if they have done these things with the paragraph they wrote in Step 2. If not, ask them to revise the paragraph.

- Tell students that there will be checklists in all of the following *Write!* sections and that they should use these to make sure they wrote their compositions correctly.

8 Editing page 8

The *Editing* activities are the grammar lessons for the unit, but they give students practice with a specific grammar point after the language need for it has been formed in the writing stage. After practicing whatever syntax is offered in this lesson, students are asked to look back at their writing to see if they used it correctly or need to make improvements.

- In this *Editing* activity, students will learn the correct format for writing a paragraph.
- Explain to students that paragraphs in English have a particular shape.
- Read the information box *Paragraph format* at the top of page 8.
- Call on a student to read one of the paragraphs at the top of page 8.

1

- Read the instructions for Step 1 aloud.
- Ask students to answer these questions and explain why they came up with those answers.
- Explain that paragraphs in print, on the Web, and in e-mail often use different rules, such as no indenting and empty lines between them, but handwritten paragraphs almost always follow these rules. Tell students that you want them to follow these rules in this course.

> **Answer**
> 1. Paragraph a is not in proper format. Paragraph b is better.

2

- Read the instructions for Step 2 aloud.
- Have students rewrite the two paragraphs in Steps 2a–b.
- Walk around the classroom, helping students as necessary.

> **Answer**
> 2. a. I enjoy my time at work. In the morning, I read letters from customers and write down their questions. Then, in the afternoon, I call these customers and answer their questions.
> b. I also enjoy my time at home. I spend a lot of time on the Internet. I can keep in touch with my friends by chatting and sending messages. In addition, I can do research for my job.

3

- Divide the class into pairs.
- Have students compare answers with a partner.

4 and 5

- Read the instructions for Steps 4 and 5 aloud.
- Have students check the paragraph they wrote in Part 7. Students who made mistakes in paragraph format should rewrite their paragraphs.
- Ask students to think about whether there is anything else they need to revise.

9 Giving feedback page 9

The *Giving feedback* activities have students read one another's writing and give feedback on the content, comprehensibility, and, to some degree, the organization. They are not asked to peer correct. The purposes of these activities are (1) to model other student's writing, (2) to make sure every writer has an audience of peers, and (3) to get them qualitative feedback on communicative competence and form.

1

- Read the instructions for Step 1 aloud.
- Divide the class into pairs.
- Tell students that they are going to check each other's paragraphs, and that they will need a sheet of paper for Step 2.
- Have students exchange paragraphs. Then read the instructions and questions for Step 1 aloud.
- You might have students put their composition inside their book and exchange that as well, so that the partner's comments are recorded in the author's book. Another option is to have readers write their comments on the back of the composition.

Unit 1 *About me* 5

- Have students complete 1a–e individually. Walk around the classroom, helping students as necessary.
- When they finish, tell students to exchange books and review their partner's answers. They can then go on to Step 2.

2
- Read the instructions for Step 2 aloud. Then call on different students to read the two example notes.
- Have students write notes to their partner like the ones in the examples.

3
- Read the instructions for Step 3 aloud.
- Have students exchange notes with their partner.

4
- Read the question in Step 4 aloud.
- Ask students to think about the question.

Just for fun page 10

Tell students they are going to do a fun activity that will help them get to know one another better.

1
- Read the instructions for Step 1 aloud.
- Ask students for ideas for additional paragraph topics, such as *foods I like to eat*, *things I like to talk about*, and *movies I like to see*.

2
- Have students follow the instructions in 2a–b.
- Walk around the classroom and help students as they are writing their paragraphs. Be sure they use correct paragraph form.
- Collect all the papers, number them, and hang them up around the room. Be sure to keep your own list indicating who wrote which paper.
- Divide the students into groups of eight if the class is large.

3
- Read the instructions for Step 3 aloud.
- Have students walk around the room reading the posted papers. Tell students to write down who they think wrote each paper in the chart.

4
- Tell students who wrote each paper.
- Ask students how many they got correct.

> *Optional activity*
> **Read it aloud**
> Select some students to read their paragraphs aloud. Have other students ask them questions.

Career consultant

Overview

In this unit, students will write a composition in which they suggest possible careers for one another based on personal work styles. First the students will interview each other on their work styles and then fill in a chart that shows what job areas their partners are best suited for. The students will then write about a career that fits their partner and explain why.

This unit introduces the basic structure of an expository composition. It builds on the ideas introduced in Unit 1. Students will learn how to use a topic sentence and how to organize a paragraph around one main idea.

Key points

- In this unit, students will learn how to organize paragraphs into a simple expository composition.
- The interview and analysis in Parts 4 and 5 are critical to the success of the unit. You should examine them in detail before class.
- Concentrate on getting your students to understand the organization of the basic paragraph, especially topic sentences and the importance of support.
- Sections can be skipped. A minimal set of sections might include Parts 4, 5, 6, and 7. You can also save time by assigning sections as homework.

1 Brainstorming page 11

1

- Refer to page 1 of this Teacher's Manual for an explanation of *brainstorming*, as needed.
- If you have already explained what brainstorming is, write the following headings on the board: *The kind of work I like* and *The kind of work I don't like*.
- Read the instructions for Step 1 aloud.
- Call on students to give examples.
- Have students brainstorm for five to ten minutes to complete their list.
- Walk around the classroom to encourage and help students.

2

- Divide the class into pairs.
- Have students compare answers with a partner.

3 and 4

- Read the instructions for Steps 3 and 4 aloud.
- Have students write down two jobs that fit them and two that don't.
- Walk around the classroom and help students as necessary.

5

- Have students compare answers with a partner.
- Elicit examples from individual students.
- Encourage students to tell you why the job is appropriate or not.

> Later in this unit . . . Call on a student to read this aloud.

> ***Optional activity***
>
> **Student survey**
>
> Have students, as a class, make a questionnaire to ask one another (or another class) which jobs are the most and least popular. List the results on the board.

2 Analyzing a paragraph page 12

This paragraph uses the development-by-division expository mode. *Division* means taking a complex topic and breaking it down into simpler parts to explain it. Students will use this mode when they write their own compositions.

1

- Read the instructions for Step 1 aloud.
- Have students read the article on their own.
- Call on students to read the article aloud, sentence by sentence.

- Have students complete Steps 1a–d individually. Say: *Remember, the topic introduces the main idea of the paragraph, but the topic sentence is not always the first sentence.*
- For 1d, you might have to explain what transition words are (also referred to as "transitional words"). Tell them that transition words are words or phrases that show how information in one sentence is connected to other sentences, and that these are very useful for showing organization. Explain how transition words like these work: *however* (to signal a difference), *therefore* (to signal a logical inference), and *first of all* (to signal the first main point in a series).
- Walk around the classroom, helping students as necessary.

> **Answers**
> 1. a. Understanding the three parts of your "personal style" might help when you decide on a career.
>   b. having friends or being successful; active or passive; feeling or thinking person
>   c. In conclusion, in addition to thinking about your interests, it is important to consider your personality when choosing a career.
>   d. *Beginning of a new subtopic:* First, Second, Third
>   *Provide more information on a subtopic:* For example, For instance

2

- Have students compare answers with a partner.
- Go over answers as a class.

> **Talk about it.** Read this aloud and have students talk with their partners for about five minutes.

3 Learning about organization page 13

- Read the information box *Supporting logical conclusions* at the top of page 13.
- Use the example to explain how logical conclusions are made from supporting ideas.
- Tell students they will have to do this in their own compositions for this unit.

1

- Read the instructions for Step 1 aloud.
- Have students complete 1a–b individually and then compare their answers in pairs.
- Go over answers as a class.

> **Answers**
> 1. a. Sandy would make a better scientist than artist.
>   b. The writing profession is a good one for Akemi.

2 and 3

- Read the instructions for Steps 2–3 aloud.
- Have students complete 2a–b and 3a–b individually and then compare their answers with a partner.
- Go over the answers as a class.

> **Answers**
> 2. a. A career as a fashion designer would be perfect for Joe.
>   *Answers will vary:*
>   Joe knows how to make good color combinations.
>   Joe is creative and artistic.
>   b. Hakim would be a good teacher.
>   *Answers will vary:*
>   Hakim knows a lot about many things.
>   Hakim is a good listener.
> 3. a. *Answers will vary:* Linda would be a good gardener.
>   b. *Answers will vary:* Carol would like a job buying and selling stocks.

4

- Read the instructions for Step 4 aloud.
- Give students an example, such as: *Keiko is wearing a new dress. Keiko has a new bag. Keiko is wearing new shoes. Keiko went shopping last weekend.*
- Have the students work in pairs to make supporting sentences and logical conclusions about their classmates. Ask them not to be negative or hurtful.
- Share some of the examples.

Optional activity

Finding the inference

Have the pairs exchange their supporting sentences with the inferences removed. Have the second pair of students try to come up with their own inference and then compare.

4 Working on content page 14

1
- Read the instructions for Step 1 aloud.
- Have students work in pairs to complete 1a–b. Explain that they must take turns interviewing each other.
- Ask a few students to share some answers to make sure everyone is on track.

2
- Read the instructions for Step 2 aloud.
- Have students take turns with their partner asking and answering the questions as they complete the chart.
- Emphasize that they should be writing their partner's responses in the chart, not their own.
- Explain vocabulary as needed (especially *physical* and *mental activities*, *being active* or *passive*).
- Explain that once in a while they might choose the third option, "not sure / like both equally," but students should try to avoid doing so. They'll get better results if they choose a preference.

Optional activity

Class chart

Draw the chart on page 14 (without the words) on the board. Elicit responses about what the class prefers for each of the nine pairs of personal characteristics. Ask for a show of hands for each and mark the chart accordingly. Tally the results for your class profile.

5 Working more on content page 15

This activity requires students to finish Part 4 on the previous page. The goal of the Part 5 activity is for students to find a career that fits their partner's personal style, based on their partner's answers in Part 4.

1
- Read the instructions for Step 1 aloud.
- Go over the example as a class.
- Have students complete the chart individually.
- Walk around the classroom, helping students as necessary.

2
- Read the instructions for Step 2 aloud.
- Have students write the job that best suits their partner.

3
- Read the instructions for Step 3 aloud.
- Brainstorm various additional jobs as a class and write them on the board.
- Have students suggest another job for their partner.

Optional activity

Guess!

Say a student's name or ask him or her to stand up. With a show of hands, ask the class to guess which of the four jobs best suits that student. Find out from the student's interviewer if the class guessed correctly.

6 Analyzing a model page 16

1
- Read the instructions for Step 1 aloud.
- Have students read the composition individually and answer questions 1a–d

> **Answers**
> 1. a. Therefore, Claudia would be a great elementary school teacher.
>   b. Claudia likes children, is good at knowing how others feel, and is trustworthy.
>   c. *Paragraph 3:*
>   Is very sensitive
>   Notices if someone is sad or not feeling well
>   Tries to cheer people up
>   *Paragraph 4:*
>   Is trustworthy and responsible
>   Always does what she says she's going to do
>   Writes down all of her appointments
>   Never misses her appointments
>   d. First of all, Second, Finally

2

- Have students compare answers in pairs.
- Call on one or more students to read the composition aloud.
- Ask students to give the answers for 1a–d.

7 Write! page 17

1 and 2

- Read the instructions for Step 1 aloud.
- Demonstrate answers for 1a–c with model answers.
- Write the following examples on the board:

I think Sarah would make a good chef.

Main idea:	Supporting points:
p2 likes cooking	often bakes cookies or other treats, reads magazines about cooking
p3 is interested in foreign food	often goes to ethnic restaurants
p4 is creative	makes her own recipes, designs her own clothes

Introductory paragraph:
Sarah likes cooking, she is interested in foreign food, and she is creative. Therefore, I think Sarah would make a good chef.

- Read the instructions for Step 2 aloud.
- Demonstrate answers for 2a–c with model answers.

- Write the following examples on the board:

Topic sentences in Step 2:
a. *Sarah likes cooking more than anything else.*
b. *She's interested in all kinds of food.*
c. *She is a very creative person.*

- Have the students complete Steps 1 and 2 individually.
- Look over their answers to make sure they understand what supporting points and topic sentences are. Help if necessary.

3 to 5

- Read the instructions for Steps 3, 4, and 5 aloud.
- Instruct students to write their compositions on a separate piece of lined paper.
- You may want to tell them to skip lines in order to make their compositions easier to edit later.
- Have students complete their composition in class or at home.
- Remind students to underline the topic sentence in each paragraph.

8 Editing page 18

Read the information box *Using the conjunctions and, but, and so* and examples at the top of page 18.

1

- Read the instructions for Step 1 aloud.
- Call on a student to read the paragraph aloud.
- Have the students complete Step 1 in class or at home.
- Go over the answers as a class.

> **Answers will vary. Possible answers:**
> 1. Yuki is a hard worker. **In addition,** she is able to finish her work independently. For example, we had a group project to do in our economics class last year. There were three people in Yuki's group. **However,** at the end of the first semester, both of her partners transferred to other schools. **As a result,** she had to do the project by herself. She worked on it in the morning, at lunchtime, **and** at night. Most people in that situation would have gone to the teacher and asked for help, **but** Yuki finished the project by herself. **Furthermore,** it was one of the best in the class. Yuki does quality work, **so** I believe she would make an excellent stockbroker.

2 and 3

- Read the instructions for Steps 2 and 3 aloud.
- If you want to focus on revising in this course, make any additional suggestions at this time.
- Have students revise their composition.

9 Giving feedback page 19

1

- Read the instructions for Step 1 aloud.
- Have students read the composition their partner wrote about them.
- You might have students put their composition inside their book and exchange that as well, so that the partner's comments are recorded in the author's book. Another option is to have readers write their comments on the back of the composition.
- Have students complete 1a–b individually. Walk around the classroom, helping students as necessary.

2

- Read the instructions for Step 2 aloud.
- Call on a student to read the letter aloud.
- Have students write their letter either in class or at home.

3 and 4

- Read the instructions for Steps 3 and 4 aloud.
- Have students give their letter to their partner.
- Ask them to discuss or write down things they could do to make their compositions better.
- Share a few of the ideas with the class.

Just for fun page 20

- Read the instructions aloud.
- Ask a student to read the sample e-mail aloud.
- Ask students if they know someone who does a job they are interested in. If not, suggest that they use company Web sites to find someone, and use that person's e-mail address, or the company's and department's regular mail address.
- Have students write regular letters or e-mail messages at home.
- Share a few of these in class.
- Tell the students to send their e-mail/letter. You may want to check them beforehand.
- Ask them to share any replies they get with the class.

> *Optional activity*
>
> **Envelope writing**
>
> Have students address their envelopes in class. Be sure that students' names and addresses are in the upper left-hand corner.

3 A dream come true

Overview

In this unit, students imagine that they are living ten years in the future and that they have become famous for their work. They take turns playing the roles of their future famous selves, and of a magazine reporter interviewing a famous person (their partner). After interviewing each other, they will write magazine articles on their partner's rise to success.

This unit introduces the expository mode of giving support with examples. Students will learn how to support topic sentences with facts and examples. It also introduces direct and indirect speech and résumé writing.

Key points

For the writing assignment, encourage students to choose great futures for themselves. Value and encourage every student's view of his or her future.

In the third paragraph of the composition, students write about positive qualities that really exist in their partners. This task should be handled with care, but if this humanistic component is managed well, it provides great rewards.

Concentrate on getting your students to understand the importance of supporting sentences.

Sections can be skipped. A minimal set of sections might include Parts 4, 5, 6, and 7. You can also save time by assigning sections as homework.

1 Brainstorming page 21

1

- Refer to page 1 of this Teacher's Manual for an explanation of *brainstorming*, as needed.
- Write the following headings on the board: *What I need to do* and *Characteristics I need to have*.
- Say: *What are some things you need to do to be successful? What are some characteristics you need?*
- Call on individual students to give examples for either category.
- Write their examples on the board.
- Have students brainstorm for five to ten minutes to complete their list.

2

- Divide the class into pairs.
- Have students compare answers with a partner and add more information to their list.

3

- Read the instructions for Step 3 aloud.
- Call on individual students to tell you the answers they circled.

> Later in this unit . . . Call on a student to read this aloud.

Optional activity

Class poll

Ask what characteristics the class thinks are the most important for success. Elicit characteristics and write them on the board. Then ask for a show of hands to see how many students have each characteristic on the lists. Find out which five characteristics are the most important.

---

2 Analyzing a paragraph page 22

This paragraph uses the development-by-example expository mode. The main ideas in the paragraph are claims, supported by facts and examples. Students will use this mode when they write their own composition.

1

- Read the instructions for Step 1 aloud.
- Have students read the paragraph individually.
- Point out that an expository paragraph uses facts and examples to explain an idea (development by example).
- Tell students that they will have to write paragraphs like this in their compositions.
- Call on students to read the paragraph aloud, sentence by sentence. Explain vocabulary, if necessary.

- Have students complete steps 1a–d individually. Say: *Remember, the topic introduces the main idea of the paragraph, but the topic sentence is not always the first sentence.*
- Walk around the classroom, helping students as necessary.

> ***Answers***
> 1. a. Anita Roddick was a successful businesswoman and also a famous environmental campaigner and human rights activist.
>   b-1. There are now more than 2,400 Body Shop stores all over the world.
>   b-2. She used her stores to teach people about the dangers of misusing the Earth.
>   b-3. She founded Children on the Edge, an organization that helps children in Eastern Europe and Asia.
>   c. In conclusion, we can see that Roddick was able to combine her personal beliefs along with her money making; this is what made her one of the world's most successful people.
>   d. *D:* "The end result of kindness is that it draws people to you."
>   *I:* She said that businesses have the power to do good.

2

- Have students compare answers with a partner.
- Go over answers as a class.
- Explain that this is a development-by-example paragraph and that students will be writing paragraphs like this in their compositions.

> **Talk about it.** Read this aloud and have students talk with their partners for about five minutes.

3 Learning about organization page 23

Read the information box *Supporting with facts and examples* at the top of page 23.

1

- Read the instructions for Step 1 aloud.
- Have students complete 1a–d individually. If students are having difficulty, do the first item together before continuing with the rest of the step.

2

- Have students compare answers with a partner.
- Elicit several examples from the students, and write them on the board.

3

- Read the instructions for Step 3 aloud.
- Have students complete Step 3 individually. Make sure they don't write embarrassing things about other students.

4

- Elicit several examples from the students.
- Write these on the board.

> ***Optional activities***
>
> **Who am I?**
>
> Write the names of famous people on pieces of paper. Attach one paper to each student's back, so he or she can't read it. Tell students to walk around asking one another questions for "support clues." They can ask *Yes/No* questions such as "Am I a famous actor?" or "Do I play baseball?" but not *Wh-* questions such as "What do I do?" or "What sport do I play?" After students have guessed their identities, they can take their paper tag off and help others.
>
> **People specs**
>
> Ask students to think of facts they know about real people, famous or not, and use them to quiz other students on who the person is. Encourage them to use quantitative information, for example: He is an African American basketball player. Experts say "he is the greatest basketball player of all time." He received five MVP awards. (Answer: Michael Jordan.) This activity works best if students have time to access the Internet.

4 Working on content page 24

Have students imagine it is ten years in the future and that they have become famous in some area. They are preparing memoirs about their rise to success.

1

- Read the instructions for Step 1 aloud.
- Tell the students that they don't have to be realistic. In fact, they shouldn't be. They should be so successful in some area that they have become national celebrities. Give them these examples:

  a doctor who found the cure for cancer

  a mother who got the prime minister's "Best Mother" award

  a company employee who became the president and revolutionized her company

  a teacher who wrote a nationally famous textbook

  a Web designer who invented 3-D sites

- Have students answer the first question individually.
- Walk around the classroom, helping students as necessary.
- Since these answers will be part of their compositions, don't have students share their answers for this or the next step.

2

- Read the instructions for Step 2 aloud.
- Go over the example.
- Have students complete the chart individually.
- Walk around the classroom, helping students as necessary.
- Encourage students to be creative and include as many events as possible, including awards, TV appearances, discoveries, study abroad, befriending key people, and so on.
- You might also suggest that students include a misstep somewhere in their rise. The more interesting information they have, the more interesting the magazine article will be.

Optional activity

Interviews

As homework, have students interview friends and family members about their successes. Students can then report on their findings in small groups or as a class.

---

5 Working more on content page 25

In this activity, students become magazine article reporters and interview the famous people made up in Part 4. The activity works best if the Step 2 and Step 3 information is hidden from the partner.

1

- Read the instructions for Step 1 aloud.
- Read the interview questions aloud.
- Put the students in pairs and assign their starting roles as reporter or famous person. The activity works better if the pairs know each other, so we suggest letting students choose their own partners.
- Have the reporters interview their partners; tell them to take extensive notes. (The space in the book might not be enough.)
- Encourage the reporters to ask follow-up questions for each answer, even if that means the famous person will have to make up additional information on the spot.
- After a while, have pairs switch roles and do the interview again.

2

- Separate the pairs so that they cannot see each other's work from now on. Don't let them see what is being written about them.
- Read the instructions for Step 2 aloud. Explain vocabulary as needed.
- Have students complete Step 2a–b individually.
- Emphasize that they should look for real characteristics in their partners, not fictitious ones.
- If pairs don't know each other very well, let them come up with more superficial characteristics, such as "a beautiful smile."
- Don't permit students to come up with characteristics that demean or embarrass their partners, even if just in joking.

3

- Read the instructions and example for Step 3 aloud.
- Have students complete 3a–b individually.
- Have them keep the answers secret from other students, especially the person being written about.

> *Optional activity*
>
> **Using a thesaurus**
>
> Divide the class into groups of three or four. Give each group a thesaurus. Ask the groups to look up some of the characteristics they have used to describe their partners and write down the synonyms. Then have each group teach the other groups at least one or two words.

6 Analyzing a model page 26

1

- Read the instructions for Step 1 aloud.
- Have students read the composition on their own.
- Call on students to read the composition aloud, paragraph by paragraph.
- Have students complete 1a–c individually.

> *Answers*
>
> 1. a. Jun-Ho is the most popular film director in our country.
>   b. Jun has been directing films since he was 18.
>   c. Jun-Ho has two characteristics that have helped make him a great director.

2

- Have students compare answers with a partner.
- Go over the answers as a class.
- Point out how facts and examples are used to support the main ideas.
- You might also point out that the second paragraph uses a different expository style: development by describing a process.

7 Write! page 27

Important point: Tell the students to keep their composition secret.

1

- Read the instructions for Step 1 aloud.
- Have students fill in the answers for Step 1 individually.
- Walk around the room and look over their answers, but don't share them as a class.

2

- Read the instructions for Step 2 aloud.
- Emphasize that (1) these are magazine articles, so they should be written in an interesting way, and (2) students should not let their partners see the article.
- Tell students to give their article a title and write their name as author. You might also have them write a relevant magazine name in the margin, such as *Business Leaders Today*.
- Note: Having students write about their partner's real strengths is a powerful but slightly risky aspect of this assignment. Monitor their choices of strengths, and ask them to write as much as they can in the third paragraph. Later, when the assignment is completed, make sure the students see what their partner wrote about them.

3

- Call on a student to read the *Writing checklist* aloud.
- Ask students to review their article and complete the checklist, either at home or in class, before turning it in.

8 Editing page 28

Read the information box *Direct and indirect speech* at the top of page 28.

1

- Read the instructions for Step 1 aloud.
- Call on individual students to read the sentences in the paragraph aloud.
- Have students work individually or in pairs to complete Step 1.
- Walk around the classroom, helping students as necessary.
- Go over the answers as a class.

> *Answer*
>
> 1. Sally Corlin says that it's her job to know the tastes of her customers.
>   She explains that she always asks them about their kids, so they see that she's really interested.
>   Frank Wang claims that it's the best shop in town.
>   He says that he recommends Sally's to all his friends.

2

- Read the instructions for Step 2 aloud.
- Have students write the two sentences.
- Walk around the classroom, helping students as necessary.
- Go over answers as a class.

3

- Read the instructions for Step 3 aloud.
- If you want to focus on revising in this course, make any additional suggestions at this time.
- Have students revise their article.

9 Giving feedback page 29

One of the great pleasures in this unit comes when students hear the positive characteristics their partner wrote about them, especially if they did not know what their partner had written beforehand. Therefore, you might opt to modify the standard procedures suggested below by collecting all the papers and reading them to the class, first, or having the authors read them. Afterward, follow these procedures.

1

- Read the instructions for Step 1 aloud.
- Have students exchange their article with their partner.
- You might have students put their composition inside their book and exchange that as well, so that the partner's comments are recorded in the author's book. Another option is to have readers write their comments on the back of the composition.
- Have students complete 1a–d individually.
- Walk around the classroom, helping students as necessary.

2

- Read the instructions for Step 2 aloud.
- Have students write their letter either in class or at home.

3 and 4

- Read the instructions for Steps 3 and 4 aloud.
- Have the students give their letter to their partner.

- Ask them to discuss or write down things they could do to make their article better.
- Share a few of the ideas with the class.
- If you haven't let the partners see them yet, collect the magazine articles. Have students submit their article with their partner's reaction letter.
- Have each student read the article written about him or her.

> **Optional activity**
> **Article display**
> Have the students write or type a final draft of their article. If possible, include photographs. Display the articles around the room, put them online, or make a booklet.

Just for fun page 30

A good résumé is important for getting a job, and design is a big part of that. We suggest you go online and download some interesting examples of résumés and use those as well.

1

- Ask: *Do you know what a résumé is?*
- Explain that a résumé is an important representation of an individual's skills and experience.
- Call on a student to read the information in Step 1 aloud.

2

- Read the instructions for Step 2 aloud.
- Have students read and study the résumé format.
- Ask a student how résumés are different in his or her country.
- Elicit responses from other students.

3

- Read the instructions for Step 3 aloud.
- Have students complete the assignment, in class or at home.

Overview

In this somewhat playful unit, students invent unusual devices, such as self-washing dishes, and write about them. They must concentrate on describing what the invention is or does and how to use it.

This unit introduces the organizational mode of definition, and teaches students how to write an attention getter (a first sentence used to attract a reader's attention). In the following units, this concept will be expanded upon to include introductory paragraphs. Writing e-mail letters is also introduced.

Key points

Encourage students to come up with humorous inventions. Be ready to capitalize on their creativity and engage in entertaining activities.

Be ready to provide additional vocabulary related to using machines (*turn on*, *knob*, *button*).

Make sure students include a picture with their composition.

Sections can be skipped. A minimal set of sections might include Parts 3, 4, 6, and 7. You can also save time by assigning sections as homework.

1 Brainstorming page 31

1

- Read the instructions for Step 1 aloud, and the examples in the list.
- Have students work alone for five to ten minutes to finish their lists.
- Walk around the classroom, helping students as necessary.

2

- Read the instructions for Step 2 aloud.
- Call on individual students for examples.
- Write the examples on the board. Develop a list of about ten to fifteen problems.

3

- Read the instructions for Step 3 aloud.
- Give students a couple of minutes to choose two problems from the list and write about them.
- Share answers with a partner.

> Later in this unit . . . Call on a student to read this aloud.

> ### Optional activity
> #### Top ten list
> Divide the class into small groups. Tell each group to make a list of the top ten most valued objects in their lives (1 being the most important, 10 being the least). Elicit answers from students and make a class chart with the results.

2 Analyzing a paragraph page 32

This paragraph uses the development-by-definition expository mode. *Definition* means telling what something means. It might include explaining what class it belongs to, its characteristics, how it is different from similar things, how it is used, and so on. Students will use this mode when they write their own composition.

1

- Read the instructions for Step 1 aloud.
- Have students read the paragraph and complete 1a–c individually.
- Call on students to read the paragraph aloud, sentence by sentence.
- Go over answers as a class.
- Explain that this is a definition paragraph and that students will be writing paragraphs like this in their compositions.
- If time permits, ask students what other things, like those in 1c, could be used to define an object, such as a smartphone, bottle of shampoo, or novel.

Unit 4 *Invent* 17

> **Answers**
> 1. a. She frequently lost things and wasted time looking for them.
>   b. Now when I can't find something, I use the Super-Finder, a small, easy-to-use electronic device that locates lost items.
>   c-1. Super-Finder
>   c-2. locates lost items
>   c-3. about the size of a small chocolate bar
>   c-4. comes in many fashionable colors

2

- Read the instructions for Step 2 aloud and have students complete the task individually.
- Go over the answers as a class.

> **Answer**
> 2. When you can't find something, all you have to do is program the Super-Finder with information about the item you are looking for. Then the Super-Finder's special detector sends a message to the item, and the item starts beeping.

> **Talk about it.** Read this aloud and have students talk with their partners for about five minutes.

> **Optional activity**
> **What is it?**
> Have students write slightly mysterious definitions without saying what the object is. Have them read these in a class guessing game.

3 Working on content page 33

1
- Read the instructions for Step 1 aloud.
- Have students work in pairs to answer the questions.
- Go over possible answers as a class.

> **Answers will vary. Possible answers:**
> 1. Love-o-meter: This measures how much someone likes you. People would use it before asking someone on a date.
>   Self-washing dish: This is used to save time and energy. Very busy or young people would use it.
>   Insta-English dictionary ring: This is used to learn English without effort. People who have difficulty remembering words, or those who are in a hurry to learn English, would use it.

2

- Read the instructions for Step 2 aloud.
- Have students complete their drawing individually.
- Walk around the classroom, helping students as necessary.
- You may wish to assign this as homework.

> **Optional activity**
> **Invention show and tell**
> Have students bring in one item that they believe is an excellent invention. It should be small and easy to carry, such as a corkscrew or an eggbeater. Have students prepare a two-minute talk about the invention, including instructions on how to use it and why it is such a great device.

4 Learning about organization page 34

Read the information box *Definition paragraphs* at the top of page 34.

1 and 2

- Read the instructions for Steps 1 and 2 aloud.
- Have the students work on the answers to Steps 1 and 2 on their own.
- Be prepared to give additional vocabulary for describing or operating devices, such as:

button	*screen*	*pull*
knob	*power cable*	*push*
handle	*battery*	*insert*
switch	*controls*	*remove*
dial	*turn on*	*record*
gauge	*adjust*	*focus*
instrument panel	*rotate*	*press*

3

- Read the instructions for Step 3 aloud.
- Have students compare inventions in pairs or small groups.

4

- Read the instructions for Step 4 aloud.
- Have students write a topic sentence as prescribed.

> **Optional activity**
>
> **Making commercials**
>
> Have students work in pairs or small groups. Let them choose one of the inventions from Part 4 to advertise. Have the group prepare a short commercial in which they introduce and describe the product. Remind them to try to "sell" the product, and introduce advertising vocabulary such as *new*, *improved*, and *the greatest*. If you have access to a video camera, tape the commercials and play them back for the class to watch.

5 Learning more about organization
page 35

Read the information box *Attention getters* at the top of page 35.

1

- Read the instructions for Step 1 aloud.
- Call on a student to tell the class the answer.

> **Answer**
> 1. quote

2

- Read the instructions for Step 2 aloud.
- Have students complete the step individually or in pairs.
- If students are having difficulty, review the first example together before continuing with the rest of the exercise.
- Have students compare answers in pairs or small groups.
- Go over answers as a class.
- Write some of the most interesting attention getters on the board.

3

- Read the instructions for Step 3 aloud and have students complete the activity.
- Call on individual students to tell the class their attention getter.

6 Analyzing a model page 36

1

- Read the instructions for Step 1 aloud.
- Have students read the composition individually.
- Call on students to read the composition aloud, paragraph by paragraph.
- Read the instructions for 1a–c aloud and have students follow the directions.

> **Answers**
> 1. a. *Attention getter:* Do you wish you could speak English better?
>   *Topic sentence:* Easy to use and effective, the Instant-English Ring is an excellent aid for learning English.
>   b. The Instant-English Ring is a special device that gives you English fluency.
>   c. The Instant-English Ring is easy to use.

2

- Have students compare answers with a partner.
- Go over answers as a class.

7 Write! page 37

1

- Read the instructions for Step 1 aloud.
- Have students complete the step individually.

2

- Read the instructions for Step 2 aloud.
- Have students write their composition. Rather than using the space in the book, you might opt to have them write it on a separate piece of lined paper.
- Tell students to skip lines so there will be room for comments. Also tell them to include a picture of their invention.
- You may want to assign the composition as homework.

3

- Call on a student to read the *Writing checklist* aloud.
- Ask students to review their composition and complete the checklist, either at home or in class, before turning it in.

8 Editing page 38

Read the information box *Avoiding repetition* at the top of page 38.

1

- Read the instructions for Step 1 aloud.
- Have students work in pairs or small groups to complete the step.
- Walk around the classroom and help students as necessary.
- Go over answers as a class.

> ***Answers*** will vary. Note that not every *memophone* should be changed to a pronoun. In fact, it is important that several remain. Possible answers:
>
> 1. **The memophone** is a device designed to send short memos. ~~The memophone~~ **It** is a box that plugs right into your telephone. Inside ~~the memophone~~ **this device** is a microphone, a computer chip, and a mini-fax. As you speak to someone on the telephone, **the memophone** listens to what you say. Anytime you tell someone to do something, ~~the memophone~~ **it** records your words and sends them as a fax to the other person's telephone. Thanks to ~~the memophone~~ **this wonderful machine**, the other person will receive a written note to remind him or her what to do. **The memophone** will keep printing out the same note every day until that person pushes ~~the memophone's~~ **its** "Done" button. **The memophone** has "Level of Importance Sensors," too. If your voice sounds urgent, **the memophone** will print the message in red ink instead of black, and ~~the memophone~~ **it** will send it once an hour instead of once a day. For example, if you call your husband and say, "You forgot to pick up the dry cleaning yesterday. Please, please, don't forget today!" **the memophone** will immediately print out a red memo saying, "Pick up dry cleaning today!" This time, thanks to ~~the memophone~~ **this helpful device**, he'll probably remember.

2 and 3

- Read the instructions for Steps 2 and 3 aloud.
- If you want to focus on revising in this course, make any additional suggestions at this time.
- Have students revise their composition.

> **Optional activity**
>
> **Discussion**
>
> Have students discuss the memophone in small groups. Write the following questions for discussion on the board: *What do you use to remind yourself or others of things that need to get done? How could the memophone change your life? What would you use it for?*

9 Giving feedback page 39

Say: *We're going to work in small groups to review our class inventions.* Divide the class into groups of four.

1

- Read the instructions for Step 1 aloud.
- Call on individual students to read 1a–e.
- Have students exchange compositions and complete 1a–b independently.
- You might have students put their composition inside their book and exchange that as well, so that the partner's comments are recorded in the author's book. Another option is to have readers write their comments on the back of the composition.
- Have students work in groups to complete 1c–d.
- Read 1e aloud.
- Call on a representative from each group to tell the class about the invention that the group chose.

2

- Read the instructions for Step 2 aloud.
- Have students write their note or e-mail either in class or at home.

3 and 4

- Read the instructions for Steps 3 and 4 aloud.
- Have the students give their note or e-mail to the inventor.
- Ask students to discuss or write down things they could do to make their composition better.
- Share a few of the ideas with the class.

20 Unit 4 *Invent*

> **Optional activity**
>
> **Art gallery**
>
> Have students write or type a final draft of their composition. Display the compositions and drawings around the classroom or hallway.

Just for fun page 40

Say: *We've been working on giving feedback to each other. Now we are going to work on giving feedback to a company.*

1
- Call on a student to read the information in Step 1 aloud.
- Explain that students should choose a company in an English-speaking country so that they can write their e-mail in English.

2
- Read the instructions for Step 2 aloud.
- Have a student read the e-mail aloud.
- Explain the parts of the e-mail.

3
- Read the instructions for Step 3 aloud.
- Tell students that they will need to choose a question, a problem, or a reason for appreciation for the content of their e-mail.
- Have students complete the assignment, look up the e-mail address (or regular mail address of the company; address letter to "Customer Service"), and send their e-mail. You may want to proofread the e-mails before they are sent.
- Have students bring in any responses they receive.

5 It changed my life!

Overview

In this unit, students are asked to think about major life events that have led to their personal growth. They choose one event to write about in a cause-and-effect composition. They write about what they were like before the event, what happened, and how they changed.

This unit introduces the expository organizational mode of Cause and Effect. It teaches students how to write introductory paragraphs, which are also powerful tools for organizing compositions. In the optional final lesson, they will also write greeting cards.

Key points

Make a special effort to create a classroom environment that encourages self-disclosure.

Students may be interested in the wisdom and developmental insights in each other's compositions, so you may want to schedule some time for sharing.

Emphasize that introductory paragraphs are excellent tools for organizing writing.

Sections can be skipped. A minimal set of lessons might include Parts 3, 5, 6, and 7. You can also save time by assigning some sections as homework.

1 Brainstorming page 41

1
- Read the instructions for Step 1 aloud.
- Have students brainstorm individually for five to ten minutes to complete their list.

2
- Read instructions for Step 2 aloud.
- Say: *Take a couple of minutes to review your list and decide which events taught you something valuable.*

3
- Read the instructions for Step 3 aloud.
- Review vocabulary as needed.
- Have students work with partners to complete Step 3.
- Share a few of their answers with the class.

> Later in this unit . . . Call on a student to read this aloud.

> *Optional activity*
> **Switching partners**
> Have students change partners and do Step 3 again. Tell them that the listening partner should ask at least one question.

2 Analyzing a paragraph page 42

This paragraph uses the cause-and-effect expository mode. Events and the resulting changes caused by those events are analyzed and described. Students will use this mode when they write their own composition. Note that this is a true story from one of our students.

1
- Read the instructions for Step 1 aloud.
- Have students read the paragraph on their own and complete 1a–d when done.

Answers

1. a. (1) selfish, (2) fire, (3) lost everything in fire, (4) hard time, (5) new appreciation
   b. It's shocking.
   c. Although I lost many things in the fire, the experience helped me to grow up.
   d. *Before the fire:* Before the fire, I was selfish. I always complained to my mother about how small my room was or how few clothes I had. I never thought about her troubles, just my own.
   What happened to the author: Then the fire happened, and it destroyed everything we owned. We were suddenly poor and had to borrow everything, even food.
   How the event changed the author: At first, I had a hard time, but slowly I began to realize that I didn't really need my old things. I just needed my family. After all, you can get new clothes anytime, but a family can never be replaced. It is true that the fire took many good things from me, but it gave me something, too. It taught me to appreciate people more than things.

2

- Have students compare answers with a partner.
- Call on students to read the paragraph aloud, sentence by sentence.
- Go over the answers as a class.
- Explain that this is a cause-and-effect paragraph and that they will be writing paragraphs like this in their compositions.
- If time permits, ask students the possible causes of other things, such as the high prices in a certain restaurant, why they bought something recently, or why they are getting better (or worse) in English.

Talk about it. Read this aloud and have students talk with their partners for about five minutes.

3 Working on content page 43

1

- Read the instructions for Step 1 aloud.
- Have students look back on their brainstorming list to complete Step 1 on their own.

2

- Read the instructions for Step 2 aloud.
- Have students complete the step with their group.

3

- Read the instructions for Step 3 aloud.
- Allow students no more than two minutes to discuss.

4

- Read the instructions for Step 4 aloud.
- Have students complete the step individually.
- Walk around the classroom and help as necessary.
- You may want to assign this as homework.

4 Learning about organization page 44

Read the information box *Cause-and-effect paragraphs* at the top of page 44.

1

- Read the instructions for Step 1 aloud.
- Have students complete 1a–e individually.
- Ask them to compare their answers with a partner.

Answers will vary. Possible answers:

1. a. I've always enjoyed watching television shows from the United States, so I like English.
   b. I really need to improve my writing. Therefore, I am taking this class.
   c. Because I loved to play sports when I was little, now I love to watch my kids play them.
   d. I have never been good at managing a budget. As a result, it is hard for me to save money.
   e. I am a student. Therefore, studying is part of my job!

2

- Read the instructions for Step 2 aloud.
- Have students complete the step individually.
- Walk around the classroom and help as necessary.
- You may want to assign this as homework.

5 Learning more about organization
page 45

Read the information box *Introductory paragraphs* at the top of page 45.

1
- Read the instructions for Step 1 aloud.
- Have students complete 1a–f individually.
- Go over answers as a class.

> **Answers**
> 1. Paragraph 1: a, c, e
>   Paragraph 2: b, d, f

2
- Read the instructions for Step 2 aloud.
- Have students work independently for several minutes to complete the step.

> **Answers for 2**
>
> | | Attention getter | Main idea | Guide |
> |---|---|---|---|
> | Paragraph 1 | c | e | a |
> | Paragraph 2 | d | b | f |

3
- Divide the class into pairs.
- Have students compare answers with a partner.

6 Analyzing a model page 46

Note that this is a true story from one of our students.

1
- Read the instructions for Step 1 aloud.
- Have students read the composition individually.
- Call on students to read the composition aloud, paragraph by paragraph.
- Read the instructions for 1a–b aloud and have students follow the directions.

> **Answers**
> 1. a. *Attention getter:* Have you ever thought that you knew someone very well and then found out that you hardly knew that person at all?
>   *Main idea:* I thought I knew him well, until one day something happened that changed my attitude toward him.
>   *Guide:* Let me explain how I used to see my father, what happened, and how it changed me.
>   b. 3: the event (what happened)
>   4: after the event (how I changed)
>   2: before the event (what I used to be like)

2
- Have students compare answers.
- Go over answers as a class.

7 Write! page 47

1
- Read the instructions for Step 1 aloud.
- Have students work individually to complete the step.

2
- Read the instructions for Step 2 aloud.
- Have students complete Step 2 individually.

3
- Read the instructions for Step 3 aloud.
- Have students write their composition on a separate piece of lined paper. Tell them to skip lines so that there will be room for comments and revisions.
- You may want to assign the composition as homework.

4
- Call on a student to read the *Writing checklist* aloud.
- Ask students to review their composition and complete the checklist, either at home or in class, before turning it in.

8 Editing page 48

Read the information box *Cause and effect* at the top of page 48.

1

- Read the instructions for Step 1 aloud.
- Emphasize that in some cases the answer will be one sentence, but in other cases it will be two.
- Have students work in pairs to complete 1a–g.
- Walk around the classroom, helping students as necessary.
- Go over answers as a class.

Answers may vary. Possible answers:

1. a. There was nowhere to sit because it was really crowded.
   b. The economy was getting worse. Therefore, few companies were hiring workers.
   c. I quit my job because I wanted to be a full-time professional musician.
   d. My father cannot walk due to a car accident when he was 30.
   e. Since my aunt often scolded me, I didn't like her very much.
   f. My sister and I could not agree. As a result, we argued over little things.
   g. My family moved to a foreign country, so I learned a new language.

2

- Read the instructions for Step 2 aloud.
- You may want to have the students show you the changes by underlining the cause-and-effect words.

3

- Read the instructions for Step 3 aloud.
- If you want to focus on revising in this course, make any additional suggestions at this time.
- Have students revise their composition.

Optional activity

Create your own exercise

Have students work in pairs to write an exercise similar to Step 1. First, tell them to write five pairs of completed sentences with the cause-and-effect words in parentheses. Then, have each pair of students exchange the sentences with another pair. Write the best examples on the board.

---

9 Giving feedback page 49

Say: *We're going to work in small groups to review our compositions.* Divide the class into groups of four.

1

- Read the instructions for Step 1 aloud.
- Call on individual students to read 1a–b aloud.
- Have each student evaluate another student's composition.
- You might have students put their composition inside their book and exchange that as well, so that the partner's comments are recorded in the author's book. Another option is to have readers write their comments on the back of the composition.
- Have groups exchange their compositions and complete 1c individually.
- Have each group give you their favorite composition.

2

- Read the instructions for Step 2 aloud.
- Ask the students with stars on their papers to read their composition to the class.
- Have students write a "lesson of life" that corresponds with each composition.
- Have students compare their lessons of life with a partner.

3

- Review the lessons of life as a class.
- Write several examples on the board.

4

- Read the instructions for Step 4 aloud.
- Return students' compositions.
- Have students share a few ideas with the class.

Unit 5 *It changed my life!* 25

> **Optional activity**
>
> **Proverbs**
>
> Have students make up proverbs based on the events and lessons of life, for example, "Nothing makes you appreciate your family like a fire." Have students write their proverbs in big, clear letters on sheets of colored paper and post them around the classroom.

Just for fun page 50

For this activity, you may want to bring in a collection of greeting cards to show to students.

1
- Read the questions in Step 1 aloud.
- Note students' responses on the board.

2
- Read Step 2 aloud.
- Elicit responses. Write any additional occasions on the board.

3
- Read Step 3 aloud.
- Have students evaluate the cards with a partner.
- Say: *Which card do you like best?* Have the class indicate their favorite by raising their hands.
- Keep a tally on the board.

4
- Read the instructions and questions for Step 4 aloud.
- Have students complete 4a–c individually.

5
- Distribute card-making supplies, such as white card stock, markers, construction paper, scissors, and glue.
- Have students design their cards in class. Or you may prefer to have them design their cards at home.
- Display the finished cards around the class before the students give them away.

Exciting destinations

Overview

In this unit, students plan one-day tours to famous resort cities and write guidebook articles about them. In order to do so, they are encouraged to use outside references and write in a guidebook style.

This unit introduces the expository organizational mode of process. It also trains students in making suggestions and using more descriptive modifiers in order to write in a guidebook style. In the final lesson, students will also learn how to use outside sources to study travel locations and write travel tips.

Key points

Encourage students to choose locations to write about that they would really like to visit someday. Monitor their choices to reduce redundancy and provide a wide variety of destinations.

Consider grouping students who are working on the same cities, or by geographical area.

Make sure students know how to format a reference and how to include their sources in the final composition.

Sections can be skipped. A minimal set of sections might include Parts 4, 5, 6, and 7. You can also save time by assigning some sections as homework.

1 Brainstorming page 51

1
- Read the instructions for Step 1 aloud.
- Have students brainstorm individually five to ten minutes to complete their list.

2
- Read the instructions for Step 2 aloud.
- Say: *Take a couple of minutes to review your list and decide which places and activities were the most memorable.*

3
- Read the instructions for Step 3 aloud.
- Have students compare travel experiences with a partner.

> Later in this unit . . . Call on a student to read this aloud.

> *Optional activity*
>
> **Class tour plans**
>
> On the board make two columns under these headings:
>
> *Places I would like   Things I would like*
> *to visit   to do there*
>
> Elicit ideas from students to complete the class chart.

2 Analyzing a paragraph page 52

This paragraph uses the process expository mode, which is sometimes a narrative mode as well. Events and actions are arranged in chronological order. Students will use this mode when they write their own composition.

1
- Read the instructions for Step 1 aloud.
- Have students read the paragraph and complete 1a–d individually.

> *Answers*
>
> 1. a. *Attention getter:* Imagine standing under Big Ben or walking through Piccadilly Circus.
>   b. *Topic sentence:* To see as much as you can during your visit, you must plan your trip carefully.
>   c. *Subtopics:* gather information, make a list, learn about the underground train lines, write down your travel plans
>   d. *Transitional phrases:* First, Next, After that, Finally

Unit 6 *Exciting destinations* 27

2

- Divide the class into pairs and have students compare answers.
- Call on students to read the paragraph aloud, sentence by sentence.
- Go over the answers as a class.
- Explain that this is a process paragraph, and that students will be writing paragraphs like this in their own composition.
- If time permits, ask students the processes of other things, such as the process of what they do in the morning before coming to school, the process of completing a homework assignment, or the process of getting married.

> **Talk about it.** Read this aloud and have students talk with their partners for about five minutes.

> *Optional activity*
>
> **Scrambled paragraphs**
>
> Have students work in small groups. Each group should write a process paragraph using transition time expressions. Give each group enough pre-cut strips of paper to write each sentence of their paragraph on a separate strip, but tell them to leave a blank in place of the time expression. Have groups switch their strips with another group, and try to put the sentences in the original order. They should also guess the missing time expressions and write them in the blanks. When they finish, have them check their results against the original paragraphs.

3 Learning about organization   page 53

Read the information box *Suggestions* at the top of page 53.

1

- Read the instructions for Step 1 aloud.
- Call on a student to read the examples in 1a.
- Remind students that there are several options.
- Have students complete 1b–g individually.
- Go over answers as a class.

> *Answers will vary. Possible answers:*
> 1. a. If you go to Paris, be sure not to miss the Louvre.
>   b. While you're in Tokyo, you should visit the Meiji Shrine.
>   c. While you're in Sydney, you might want to see Bondi Beach.
>   d. If you go to London, a visit to Buckingham Palace is a must.
>   e. While you're in Egypt, it's essential that you see the pyramids.
>   f. If you go to New York, try to visit Central Park.
>   g. While you're in Peru, it would be a good idea to visit Machu Picchu.

2

- Read the instructions for Step 2 aloud.
- Have students write two suggestions.
- You may want to have them make one strong suggestion and one weaker one.

3

- Have students compare answers with a partner.
- Go over answers as a class.

> *Optional activity*
>
> **Recommendation list**
>
> Say: *What places should we suggest to visitors?* Write a list of places on the board. Then call on students to make sentence suggestions.

4 Working on content   page 54

1

- Read the instructions for Step 1 aloud.
- Allow students a couple of minutes to look over the map and indicate where they have been or would like to go.
- Elicit responses from the class. Say: *Where have you been? Where would you like to go?*
- Write two columns on the board:
  Places we've been   *Places we'd like to go*
- Write students' answers in the columns.

28   Unit 6 *Exciting destinations*

2

- Read the instructions for Step 2 aloud.
- Give students a few minutes to think about the city they chose.

3

- Read the instructions for Step 3 aloud.
- Bring in a variety of books and magazines for the students to use as resources.
- You may choose to send students to the library or have them use computers to do research.
- This step can be completed in class or at home.

4

- Read the explanation in Step 4 aloud.
- Have students spend a few minutes reviewing the chart.
- Answer any questions.

5

- Read the instructions for Step 5 aloud.
- Have students complete the step individually.
- Refer students to the examples in Step 4.
- You may choose to assign this step as homework.

5 Learning more about organization
page 55

Read the information box *Process paragraphs* at the top of page 55.

- Read the instructions at the top of page 55 aloud.
- Call on students to read the questions aloud.
- Elicit possible answers from students.
- You may want to model the task first by making an itinerary for your own city. Copy the itinerary chart onto the board. Call on students to help fill it in.
- Tell the students to write their own itinerary. Explain that they don't need to write a separate activity for each hour. Three major activities will be enough.
- If some students have chosen the same city, you may want to group them together and have them write different itineraries.
- You might even assign groups of students to the same cities for this purpose.
- Walk around the classroom, helping students as necessary.

Optional activity

School tour

Write on the board: *Itinerary*. Ask students to help you write an itinerary for a visitor to your school. Begin with the school's starting time. Elicit suggestions from students and write them on the board. Remind students to use the language for making suggestions that they learned in Part 3.

---

6 Analyzing a model page 56

1

- Read the instructions for Step 1 aloud.
- Have students read the composition individually.
- Call on students to read the composition aloud, paragraph by paragraph.
- Read the instructions for 1a–c aloud and have students follow the directions.

Answers

1. a. *Attention getter:* Let's visit a city built on dreams!
   Main idea: Here's a one-day tour of one of America's most fantastic cities: Las Vegas.
   Guide: You'll start the day with a visit to a unique shopping center, then go to a first-class restaurant, and finally end the tour next to a sinking ship.

   b. *Second paragraph:* (shopping in) the Forum Shops
   Third paragraph: (eating at) Trevi's
   Fourth paragraph: (seeing the) Treasure Island Casino show

   c. *Answers will vary. Possible answers:*
   restful night
   magnificent Caesar's Palace
   most unusual shopping mall
   Interesting shops
   most delicious Italian food
   steaming cup of cappuccino
   amazing show

Unit 6 *Exciting destinations* 29

2
- Have students compare answers.
- Go over answers as a class.

7 Write! page 57

1
- Read the instructions for Step 1 aloud.
- Have students complete their introductory paragraph in the space provided.

2
- Read the instructions for Step 2 aloud.
- Have students draft their topic sentences in the spaces provided.

3
- Read the instructions for Step 3 aloud.
- Have students write their composition on a separate piece of lined paper. Tell them to skip lines so that there will be room for comments and revisions.
- You may want to assign the composition as homework.

4
- Call on a student to read the *Writing checklist* aloud.
- Remind students to check their composition against this list before they turn in their paper.
- After you finish the other lessons in this unit, you might opt to put the compositions together in a guidebook.

8 Editing page 58

Read the information box *Using modifiers* at the top of page 58.

1
- Read the instructions for Step 1 aloud.
- Review the vocabulary as needed.
- Have students work with a partner or in small groups to complete 1a–f.
- Walk around the classroom, helping students as necessary.
- Go over answers as a class.

> *Answers will vary. Possible answers:*
> 1. a. New York City is known for its dramatic skyline.
>   b. Busy people walk down the bustling streets.
>   c. Exotic shops in Chinatown sell appetizing food.
>   d. Tourists love the breathtaking view from the top of the Empire State Building.
>   e. Riding New York's affordable subway is an adventure.
>   f. The exciting nightlife is famous all over the world.

2
- Read the instructions for Step 2 aloud.
- Have students rewrite three sentences from their composition using modifiers.

3
- Read the instructions for Step 3 aloud.
- Have students revise their composition.

> **Optional activity**
> **Using a thesaurus**
> Obtain several copies of a thesaurus. In groups, have students write the two headings *great* and *terrible* on a piece of paper. Then have them use a thesaurus to find ten other words with the same meanings. Tell them to write the words in the columns. Elicit examples from the class and write them on the board. You may want to ask students to use the words in sentences.

9 Giving feedback page 59

1
- Read the instructions for Step 1 aloud.
- Have students exchange their compositions and complete 1a–b individually.
- The group members do not need to agree with one another on their answers.
- Elicit responses from the class.

30 Unit 6 *Exciting destinations*

2 and 3

- Read the instructions for Step 2 aloud.
- Have students complete their postcard individually.
- Have students take turns reading their card aloud.
- For Step 3, have students review their composition and share any ideas they have for changes.

> **Optional activity**
>
> **Tour-agency role play**
>
> Group the students by cities in geographical areas. Each group will be a tour agency selling tours to that area. Have students brief one another on their tours, decide prices for each, and make signs or posters for their company. Then set up the tour companies around the classroom. Have half the students run their companies, while the other half act as customers, walking around and signing up for tours. After 15 to 20 minutes, have students switch roles.

Just for fun page 60

Have students work in pairs.

1

- Read the instructions for Step 1 aloud.
- Ask each pair to choose a tour destination.
- As they do so, write their choices on the board so that other pairs don't choose the same places.

2

- Read the instructions for Step 2 aloud.
- Ask the pairs to research their destination and write their top ten travel tips.
- Assign this as homework, if possible, so that they can use Internet resources.

3

- Have the student pairs post their list of travel tips on their desks.
- While one member stays and reads the tips to visitors, the other will walk around and look at other student tips.

7 Classifying classmates

Overview

In this unit, students conduct simple research on their classmates by choosing a research question and surveying them. The "interviewers" analyze the results by classifying the respondents into groups and then describe these groups and their responses in a composition.

This unit introduces the expository organizational mode of classification. Students are also taught how to write concluding paragraphs and how to use commas. They will learn to write and deliver oral presentations in the optional final lesson.

Key points

Make sure students choose good research questions to ask their classmates. The questions should be interesting and should lead to a variety of responses, but they should also allow the respondents to be classified into groups. Questions such as "When is your birthday?" probably will not lead to very interesting compositions.

Emphasize that there are many ways to classify objects into groups, and that in choosing a system of classification, the purpose and audience should be taken into consideration.

Point out the importance of concluding paragraphs for giving closure to writing. Three types of conclusions are illustrated here – summaries, predictions, and evaluations – but other types exist as well.

Sections can be skipped. A minimal set of sections might include Parts 3, 4, 5, 6, and 7. You can also save time by assigning sections as homework.

1 Brainstorming page 61

1
- Read the instructions for Step 1 aloud.
- Have students brainstorm on their own for five to ten minutes to complete their list.

2
- Read the instructions for Step 2 aloud.
- Say: *Take a couple of minutes to review your list with your partner and add more items to your own list.*

- Review the answers as a class by asking students what questions they have on their list.
- Write the heading *Questions I'd like to ask* on the board, with examples from the students underneath.

> Later in this unit . . . Call on a student to read this aloud.

> ### Optional activity
> **Scrambled polite questions**
>
> Elicit ways to make questions more polite in English. Write the following questions on the board. Teach students any of these forms and expressions they don't mention.
>
> *May I ask you a personal question? What are your plans for the future?*
>
> *Could you tell me what your plans are for the future?*
>
> *Would you mind telling me what your plans are for the future?*
>
> *Would you mind if I asked you what your plans are for the future?*
>
> Stress that word order is different in polite questions. Then give students scrambled versions of complete polite questions to put in order. This can be done as a group race.

2 Analyzing a paragraph page 62

This paragraph uses the development-by-classification expository mode. A large number of items are classified into groupings to make them easier to explain. The groupings should fit the informational needs of the audience. Students will use this mode when they write their own composition.

1
- Read the instructions for Step 1 aloud.
- Have students read the paragraph and complete 1a–d individually.

Answers

1. a. *Topic sentence:* The psychologist studied how husbands and wives got along and found that there are three types of couples.
   b. *Attention getter:* How can you find out if you and your partner are likely to be a good couple?
   c. *Subtopics:* calm-calm couples, passionate-passionate couples, calm-passionate couples
   d. In contrast – It introduces a difference.
      Interestingly – It introduces something unexpected and interesting.
      As a result – It follows a cause and introduces an effect.
      Of course – It introduces a fact that most people know.

2

- Divide the class into pairs and have students compare answers.
- Call on students to read the paragraph aloud, sentence by sentence.
- Go over the answers as a class.
- Explain that this is a classification paragraph and that students will be writing paragraphs like this in their compositions.

3

- Read Step 3 aloud and have students discuss their answers with their partner.
- Go over answers as a class.
- If time permits, ask students to classify other things into groups, such as the kinds of books they have, types of flowers, or main dishes in the cafeteria.

Talk about it. Read this aloud and have students talk with their partners for about five minutes.

Optional activity

More couple types

Have students make up their own classifications of couples, and conduct an informal survey of what they think the best combination of personality types would be.

3 Learning about organization page 63

Read the information box *Classification paragraphs* at the top of page 63.

1

- Read the instructions for Step 1 aloud.
- Call on students to read the instructions for 1a–d aloud.
- Have students work with a partner or in small groups to complete 1a–d.
- Remind students that there are many possible answers.

Answers will vary. Possible answers:

1. a. Groups based on kinds of food: Appetizers, Main Dishes, Beverages
   b. Groups based on size: Small, Medium, Large
   c. Groups based on free time: Playing Soccer, Reading, Gardening
   d. Groups based on future plans: Learning English, Finishing College, Starting a Business

2

- Have students compare answers with a partner, or in small groups.
- Go over answers as a class.

Optional activity

Classification

Bring to class a large assortment of international postage stamps or coins. Have students work in groups to find as many ways as they can to classify the items. After giving them some discussion time, go over each group's categories as a class. Some sample classifications for postage stamps might be:

stamps with people on them
stamps from Asia
stamps that are in a sheet of stamps
stamps that have been canceled

Point out to students that there are many ways to classify items and that this is an exercise in creative thinking.

4 Working on content page 64

1
- Read the instructions for Step 1 aloud.
- Call on students to read the questions aloud.
- Give students a few minutes to think about and write their answers individually.
- Have students write their research question individually.
- Be sure they choose a question that will get a variety of responses that can be classified into groups.

2
- Read the instructions for Step 2 aloud.
- Have students write their question and responses on a separate piece of paper.
- After students begin asking each other questions, walk around and help as necessary.

3
- Read the instructions for Step 3 aloud.
- Have students fill in their charts individually.
- Give students time to analyze the results and help as necessary.
- You may want to have students complete this for homework.

4
- Read the instructions for Step 4 aloud.
- Have students work with a partner for several minutes to discuss their answers, why they chose them, and other ways of classifying their classmates.
- Ask for volunteers to share their research questions and responses with the class.

> **Optional activity**
>
> **Survey results poster**
>
> After students finish their survey, have them make a poster describing the results. Bring in poster board, markers, old magazines, and glue. Encourage students to use charts, graphs, and icons. Put students' posters up in the classroom. After they finish their composition in Part 7, students can post their composition next to their poster to serve as an illustration.

5 Learning more about organization page 65

Read the information box *Concluding paragraphs* at the top of page 65.

1
- Read the instructions for Step 1 aloud.
- Have students work individually to complete the step.

> **Answers**
> 1. Paragraph A: summary
>   Paragraph B: evaluation
>   Paragraph C: prediction

2
- Have students compare answers with a partner.
- Go over answers as a class.

6 Analyzing a model page 66

1
- Read the instructions for Step 1 aloud.
- Have students read the composition individually.
- Call on students to read the composition aloud, paragraph by paragraph.
- Read the instructions for 1a–c aloud and have students follow the directions.

> **Answers**
> 1. a. Three parts of the introduction:
>   (1) Where will everyone be next year after they graduate? Will they return to their own countries or stay abroad?
>   (2) To find out, I conducted a survey. I asked each of my classmates what he or she plans to do after graduating.
>   (3) After looking over their answers, I realized that there are three types of students in the class: the "Don't Know" type, the "Go Back Home" type, and the "Stay Abroad" type.
>   b. Paragraph 2: "Don't Know" types
>   Paragraph 3: "Go Back Home" types
>   Paragraph 4: "Stay Abroad" types
>   c. prediction

2

- Have students compare answers with a partner.
- Go over answers as a class.

7 Write! page 67

1 and 2

- Read the instructions for Steps 1 and 2 aloud.
- Have students write their topic sentences and concluding paragraph.
- Monitor and help students as necessary.

3

- Read the instructions for Step 3 aloud.
- Have students write their composition on a separate piece of lined paper. Tell them to skip lines so that there will be room for comments and revisions.
- You may want to assign the composition as homework.

4

- Read the instructions for Step 4 aloud.
- Call on a student to read the *Writing checklist* aloud.
- Remind students to check their composition against this list before they turn it in.

8 Editing page 68

Read the information box *Using commas* at the top of page 68.

1

- Read the instructions for Step 1 aloud.
- Point out the first sentence, in which two commas have already been added.
- Have students work individually or with a partner to complete the step.
- Walk around the classroom, helping students as necessary.
- Go over answers as a class.

Answers

1. Campus fashions might change, but the basic college student is always the same, right? [2] Wrong! College students in universities all over the world have changed a lot in the last 30 years, and we can expect these changes to continue. [1] First of all, whereas college students used to be fairly young, almost all aged between 18 and 22, they are now much older. [3] In the United States, for example, some reports show that there are more college students older than 22 than younger! [2] In addition, today's students are doing more things than before. [1] Thirty years ago, almost all college students went to school full-time, taking three or more classes. [2] They just studied. Today, however, there are more students going part-time than full-time. [2] In addition to studying, they are also working at jobs, managing finances, and taking care of children. [3] In conclusion, college students are not staying the same; they are changing. [1] In fact, they are changing almost as quickly as campus fashions! [1]

2

- Read the instructions for Step 2 aloud.
- Allow students several minutes to review comma usage in their composition.

3

- Read the instructions for Step 3 aloud.
- If you want to focus on revising in this course, make any additional suggestions at this time.
- Have students revise their composition.

> **Optional activity**
>
> **More comma practice**
>
> Retype a paragraph from a reading book at your students' level, omitting all the commas. Tell students how many commas are missing from the paragraph and have them put the commas in the places they think are appropriate. Go over answers as a class.

9 Giving feedback page 69

Divide the class into pairs.

1
- Read the instructions for Step 1 aloud.
- Have students exchange their compositions and complete 1a–f individually.
- You might have students put their composition inside their book and exchange that as well, so that the partner's comments are recorded in the author's book. Another option is to have readers write their comments on the back of the composition.

2
- Read the instructions for Step 2 aloud.
- Call on a student to read the example note aloud.
- Have students write their letter individually.

3
- Read the instructions for Step 3 aloud.
- Give students a moment to exchange notes.

4
- Read the instructions for Step 4 aloud.
- Give the students several minutes to revise their composition.

Optional activity

Giving opinions

Pass out copies of a short news article based on a survey. Have students read the article individually and discuss their reactions in groups. Elicit responses from the groups to discuss as a class.

Just for fun page 70

1
- Read the instructions for Step 1 aloud.
- Read 1a–c aloud, and call on students to read the examples.

2
- Read the instructions for Step 2, including 2a–c, aloud.
- Have students complete 2a–c individually.
- Walk around the classroom and help as needed.

3
- Read the instructions for Step 3 aloud.
- Let students think about what they can do to improve their presentation.
- Have them practice their presentation. When practicing, have them stand up, face the wall and practice using their voice and eyes. Gestures, timing, eye contact, and voice projection are just as important to learn as the words.
- When they are ready, have students deliver their presentation to the class.

8 The job interview

Overview

In this unit, students will write a composition about how to succeed in a job interview. In order to get information for their composition, they will discuss interviewing with their classmates and do "good interview" vs. "bad interview" role plays.

This unit introduces the expository organizational mode of comparison and contrast. Students are trained in using comparative words, and adjusting the strength of a suggestion by using different verbs. They will also talk to experts on job-interviewing techniques in the optional final lesson.

Key points

If the role plays are set up properly, this unit will not only provide students with information useful to their lives, but it will also be rather humorous.

Be sure to define specific jobs for which the students will be writing job interviews.

Make sure students organize the writing for their composition in a way that leads to comparison and contrast.

Sections can be skipped. A minimal set of sections might include Parts 4, 5, 6, and 7. You can also save time by assigning sections as homework.

1 Brainstorming page 71

1

- Write *DOs* and *DON'Ts* on the board. Ask students if they know what these words mean.
- Explain that in English, when we talk about DOs and DON'Ts, we mean things that we should do and shouldn't do.
- Read the instructions for Step 1 aloud.
- Call on a student to read the examples in the book.
- Have students brainstorm individually for five to ten minutes to complete their list.

2

- Read the instructions for Step 2 aloud.
- Have students compare answers with a partner and add more information to their list.

3

- Read the questions and instructions for Step 3 aloud. Say: *Take a couple of minutes to review your list and pick your choices for the best and worst things to do in an interview.*
- Go over some of the answers as a class.

> Later in this unit . . . Call on a student to read this aloud.

2 Analyzing a paragraph page 72

This paragraph uses the development-by-comparison-and-contrast expository mode. The similarities and differences of two things are compared in order to define and separate them. Students will use this mode when they write their own composition.

1

- Read the instructions for Step 1 aloud.
- Have students read the paragraph on their own and complete 1a–d when done.

> *Answers*
> 1. a. *Topic sentence:* I have two bosses, Michelle and Eliza, and I think Michelle is better.
>   b. Michelle and Eliza
>   c. feedback, time, trust
>   d. on the other hand – It shows a contrast.
>   However – It shows a contrast.
>   Furthermore – It shows more information will be added to the previous point.
>   In conclusion – It shows a conclusion.

2

- Divide the class into pairs and have the students compare answers.
- Call on students to read the paragraph aloud, sentence by sentence.
- Go over the answers as a class.

- Explain that this is a comparison-and-contrast paragraph, and that students will be writing paragraphs like this in their own compositions.
- If time permits, ask students to compare or contrast other things, such as places they've lived, their two best friends, or two recent movies.

> **Talk about it.** Read this aloud and have students talk with their partners for about five minutes.

> *Optional activity*
>
> **Good boss/bad boss**
>
> Have students make up a survey to find out what classmates or other students think are the best/worst qualities of a boss. Compare results by making a class chart.

3 Learning about organization   page 73

Read the information box *Comparison-contrast paragraphs* at the top of page 73.

1

- Read the instructions for Step 1 aloud.
- Warn students that they may have to add information or write an additional sentence.
- Have students complete 1a–c individually.

2

- Read the instructions for Step 2 aloud.
- Have students complete the sentences individually.
- Walk around the classroom, helping students as necessary.

> *Answers will vary. Possible answers:*
>
> 2. a. Michelle always encourages me. Eliza, however, never encourages me.
>   b. Eliza never takes the time to talk to me, whereas Michelle always does.
>   c. Like Eliza, Michelle always comes early.
>   d. Unlike Eliza, Michelle stays late.
>   e. While Eliza doesn't encourage me very much, Michelle does.
>   f. Both Michelle and Eliza have a lot of experience.

3

- Have students compare answers with a partner.
- Go over answers as a class.

> *Optional activity*
>
> **Apples and oranges**
>
> Divide students into pairs. Give each pair two things or people to compare and contrast. Examples may include TV and the Internet, city life and country life, domestic films and foreign films, teenagers and adults, and so on. Have students think of as many comparisons and contrasts between the two items or people as they can. This can be done as either a spoken or a written exercise.

4 Working on content   page 74

1

- Read the directions for Step 1 aloud.
- Call on a student to read the jobs in the box and explain any vocabulary as needed.
- Give students a few minutes to think about and write their answers.

2

- Divide the class into groups of three.
- Read the instructions for Step 2 aloud.
- Call on a student to read the sample interviewer's questions.
- Have students brainstorm in groups and write down possible questions.
- Elicit questions from the class and write them on the board. Don't erase the board because you will use the questions again in Part 5.
- Discuss as a class any questions that may be inappropriate for an interview and erase them from the board.

> *Answers will vary. Possible answers:*
>
> 2. What are some of your long-term goals?
>   What experience do you have in this position?
>   What is one thing you have done that you are most proud of?
>   What is your greatest weakness?

3

- Read the instructions for Step 3 aloud.
- Have students work in their groups to develop a role play.
- Walk around the classroom to encourage and help students as needed.

4

- Read the instructions for Step 4 aloud.
- After several minutes, have students switch roles and role-play again.

> **Optional activity**
>
> **Dream job**
>
> Have students write a paragraph about their dream job. Tell them to describe the job in detail. Have them share their paragraph with their group before they do the role play in Part 5. The interviewers should tailor their questions to the jobs described in the paragraphs.

5 Working more on content page 75

1

- Have students work with the same group they worked with in Part 4.
- Read the instructions for Step 1 aloud.
- Have students brainstorm a list of inappropriate responses.
- Refer to the questions on the board from Part 4. Elicit inappropriate responses from students, and write them next to the questions.

2

- Read the instructions for Step 2 aloud.
- Tell students to practice interviews with good and inappropriate responses because they're going to perform in front of the class.

3

- Read the instructions for Step 3 aloud.
- Call on the different groups to perform their role plays in front of the class.
- Have students in the audience make a list of interviewing DOs and DON'Ts individually.
- After each group, elicit from the class the DOs and DON'Ts seen in the role play.

4

- Read the questions for Step 4 aloud.
- Call on students to state their opinions.
- Have students vote on the best interview.

6 Analyzing a model page 76

1

- Read the instructions for Step 1 aloud.
- Have students read the article individually.
- Call on students to read the article aloud, paragraph by paragraph.
- Read the instructions for 1a–c aloud and have students follow the directions.

> **Answers**
>
> 1. a. *Attention getter:* My mother used to say, "If you want that job, dress like you already have it."
>
>   *Topic sentence:* First impressions are important, so wearing the right clothes to an interview can make a difference in whether or not you will get the job.
>
>   *Guide:* There are three things you must think about when choosing clothes for an interview: color, style, and comfort.
>
>   b. *Topic sentence in Paragraph 2:* The color of your clothes sends a message, so you should fit the clothes to the job.
>
>   *Topic sentence in Paragraph 3:* In addition to color, the style of your suit makes a difference.
>
>   *Topic sentence in Paragraph 4:* The last important point about choosing an outfit is whether or not it is comfortable.
>
>   c. summary

2

- Have students compare answers with a partner.
- Go over answers as a class.

7 Write! page 77

1 to 3

- Read the instructions for Steps 1–3 aloud.
- Have students complete the steps on their own.
- Walk around and help students as needed.

4

- Read the instructions for Step 4 aloud.
- Have students write their composition on a separate piece of lined paper. Tell them to skip lines so that there will be room for comments and revisions.
- You may want to assign the composition as homework.

5

- Call on a student to read the *Writing checklist* aloud.
- Remind students to check their composition against this list before they turn it in.

> **Optional activity**
>
> **Dress for success booklet**
>
> Bring in (or have students bring in) some fashion magazines for men and women. Have students work in small groups and cut out pictures of clothing they think is suitable or unsuitable for the workplace. Each group should make a booklet describing why the clothes they chose are appropriate or inappropriate.

8 Editing   page 78

Read the information box *Giving advice* at the top of page 78.

1

- Read the instructions for Step 1 aloud. Read the example.
- Have students complete 1a–k individually or with a partner.
- Walk around the classroom, helping students as necessary.
- Go over answers as a class.

> *Answers will vary. Possible answers:*
> 1. a. may want to
>   b. must not
>   c. had better/should/ought to
>   d. had better/should/ought to
>   e. shouldn't/ought not/had better not
>   f. had better/should/ought to
>   g. shouldn't/ought not/had better not
>   h. may want to
>   i. shouldn't/ought not/had better not
>   j. may want to
>   k. have to/must

2

- Read the instructions for Step 2 aloud.
- Allow students several minutes to review their composition and complete the step.

3

- Read the instructions for Step 3 aloud.
- If you want to focus on revising in this course, make any additional suggestions at this time.
- Have students revise their composition.

9 Giving feedback   page 79

Say: *We're going to work in small groups to review our compositions.* Divide the class into groups of four.

1

- Read the instructions for Step 1 aloud.
- Have students from one group exchange their compositions with members of another group and complete the step individually.
- You might have students put their composition inside their book and exchange that as well, so that the partner's comments are recorded in the author's book. Another option is to have readers write their comments on the back of the composition.

2

- Read the instructions for Step 2 aloud.
- Have students compare their notes.
- Have students discuss and decide which advice is most useful.
- Have students write the reasons in the paragraph as a group.

3

- Read the instructions for Step 3 aloud.
- Have students report back to the class.
- Call on individual representatives of the groups to read their paragraphs from Step 2.

4

- Read the instructions for Step 4 aloud.
- Have students revise their compositions.

Just for fun page 80

This DOs and DON'Ts activity involves work outside of the classroom. Students are asked to contact two professionals in order to complete this task.

1

- Read the instructions for Step 1 aloud.
- Have students complete the step before the next class.

2

- Read the instructions and example for Step 2 aloud.
- Have students look at their completed lists in Step 1 and prepare statements individually in both direct and indirect speech.
- Have students meet in groups to report their findings.

3

- Read the instructions for Step 3 aloud.
- Call on groups to present their suggestions to the class.
- You may want to have group representatives write the two most interesting suggestions on the board.

9 Personal goals

Overview

In this unit, students will write a composition about their life goals. In order to get information to write about in their compositions, they will complete two exercises in which they make lists of their future goals.

This unit introduces the concept of the persuasive mode of expository writing. Students will practice adding support – statistics, personal experiences, or quotes – to bolster their persuasive writing. They will also practice writing verb phrase parallel structures and write positive comments to one another in the optional final lesson.

Key points

Point out that, although they overlap, persuasive writing is different from expository writing. Simply put, *expository writing* means explaining, whereas *persuasive writing* means convincing.

Make sure the goals that the students set are reasonable, positive, and will require some effort to achieve. However, they should be goals that can be achieved within a few years.

Allow students to modify their goals after seeing those that other students have set.

Make special efforts to maintain a positive classroom environment.

During the final optional lesson, be sure students know that negative comments, even if they are "just joking," will not be tolerated. Tell students that if they can't find anything positive to say to someone they should not write anything.

Sections can be skipped. A minimal set of sections might include Parts 3, 4, 6, and 7. You can also save time by assigning lessons as homework.

1 Brainstorming page 81

1

- Write *Changes* and *Future goals* on the board.
- Read the instructions for Step 1 aloud.
- Call on a student to read the examples in the book aloud.
- Have students brainstorm individually for five to ten minutes to complete their lists.

2

- Read the instructions for Step 2 aloud.
- Say: *Take a couple of minutes to review your lists.*

3

- Ask students if they have any changes or goals in common with their partner.
- Write some examples on the board.

Later in this unit . . . Call on a student to read this aloud.

Optional activities

Class goal survey

Have students mingle and seek out other students with similar goals. After several minutes, call on students to tell you the goals. Write them on the board for discussion. Allow students to add to their list if they wish.

Future timelines

Have students make a time line for the next twenty years of their lives. Encourage them to be creative. Have students explain their time lines to one another in small groups. Then post the time lines on the classroom walls.

2 Analyzing a paragraph page 82

This paragraph uses a persuasive style of organization. Hypothetical claims are made and then supported by additional information. This style is often used in argumentative writing, such as essays, opinion pieces, and research papers. Students will use this style when they write their own composition.

1
- Read the instructions for Step 1 aloud.
- Have students read the paragraph on their own and complete 1a–e when done.

> *Answers*
> 1. a. Life is full of choices.
>   b. Sometimes by choosing the hard way, there is more to gain.
>   c. In short, the easy way isn't always the best way.
>   d. For example – It introduces an example.
>   However – It shows a difference.
>   In short – It shows a conclusion.
>   e. By choosing

2
- Have students compare answers with a partner.
- Call on students to read the paragraph aloud, sentence by sentence.
- Go over the answers as a class.
- Explain that this paragraph uses persuasive writing, and that students will be writing paragraphs like this in their own compositions.

> **Talk about it.** Read this aloud and have students talk with their partners for about five minutes.

> *Optional activity*
> **Mottos and examples**
> In small groups, have students write down their personal motto. Have them read their motto to the group, giving two or more examples to support it. Examples may be "Always look on the bright side of life" or "Never give up."

3 Working on content page 83

1
- Read the instructions for Step 1 aloud.
- Call on a student to read the examples aloud.
- Allow students about 10 minutes (this, of course, will vary depending on your class) to complete their charts individually.
- Walk around the classroom, helping students as necessary.

2
- Read the instructions for Step 2 aloud.
- Allow students several minutes to complete the chart with their information.
- Walk around and help students as needed.

4 Working more on content page 84

1
- Read the instructions for Step 1 aloud.
- Call on a student to read the example aloud.
- Have students complete 1a–d individually.
- Walk around the classroom, helping students as necessary.

2
- Read the instructions for Step 2 aloud.
- Have students compare answers with a partner.

3
- Read the instructions for Step 3 aloud.
- Give students time to complete the chart.
- Ask students if they have any changes or goals in common with their partner.
- Write some examples on the board.

> *Optional activity*
> **Make up a new exercise**
> Have students work in small groups to write a similar exercise for their classmates to complete.

5 Learning about organization page 85

Read the information box *Persuasive paragraphs* at the top of page 85.

1

- You may choose to have students complete Part 5 for homework in preparation for the composition they will write in Part 7.
- Read the instructions for Step 1 aloud.
- Call on students to read the examples given in each category.
- Have students complete 1a–c individually.
- Walk around the classroom to encourage and help students as necessary.

> *Answers will vary. Possible answers:*
> 1. a. If I make a new Web site for myself, I might make some new friends. After all, my brother did when he made his.
>   b. I will spend 30 minutes exercising every day. As Edward Stanley said, "Those who think they have no time for bodily exercise will sooner or later have to find time for illness."
>   c. Historians consider Ankor Wat, in Cambodia, the Rome of the East. I must visit it someday.

2

- Read the instructions for Step 2 aloud.
- Allow students several minutes to complete the step.
- Remind students that the goals they choose will be used in their composition, so they should be meaningful. Tell them that the deadline does not have to be a date. It can be a year (2012), an age (by 35), or an event (before I get married).

6 Analyzing a model page 86

1

- Read the instructions for Step 1 aloud.
- Have students read the composition individually.
- Call on students to read the composition aloud.
- Read the instructions for 1a–c aloud and have students follow the directions.

> *Answers*
> 1. a. learn Mandarin, visit China, become more organized
>   b. *Topic sentence in Paragraph 2:* First, I want to learn how to speak Mandarin Chinese.
>   *Topic sentence in Paragraph 3:* Next, I plan to save some money so that I can go to China within the next three years.
>   *Topic sentence in Paragraph 4:* Finally, I would like to become more organized and not get so overwhelmed by things that I need to do.
>   c. The author gives support for each point: research (690 million people in China . . .) quote ("A journey of a thousand miles . . .") personal experience (For example, at the beginning of every semester . . .)

2

- Have students compare answers with a partner.
- Go over answers as a class.

7 Write! page 87

1

- Read the instructions for Step 1 aloud.
- Have students complete the step individually.
- If you are in a school, you may want to have students choose goals they can complete while they are students. Set the date for opening the letters just before graduation.

2

- Read the instructions for Step 2 aloud.
- Have students complete the step individually.

3

- Read the instructions for Step 3 aloud.
- Have students write their composition on a separate piece of lined paper. Tell them to skip lines so that there will be room for comments and revisions.
- You may want to assign the composition as homework.

4

- Call on a student to read the *Writing checklist* aloud.
- Remind students to check their composition against this list before they turn it in.

5

- Read the instructions for Step 5 aloud.
- At the end of the unit, return the letters and ask the students to follow the instructions.
- Encourage students to keep these letters in a safe place until the opening date arrives.

8 Editing page 88

Read the information box *Parallel construction* at the top of page 88.

1

- Read the instructions for Step 1 aloud.
- Have students work individually or with a partner to rewrite the sentences in 1a–f.
- Walk around the classroom, helping students as necessary.
- Go over answers as a class.

> **Answers**
> 1. a. I want to start to read the newspaper every day, ~~takeing~~ **taking** long walks, and ~~visiting~~ **visiting** more with my friends.
>   b. Organizing dinners for friends, studying more, and ~~to keeping~~ **keeping** his room cleaner are just three of Taka's goals.
>   c. Rawan hopes to finish school, save some money, and ~~will start~~ **start** her own business.
>   d. Luisa wants to visit the ocean, start speaking English every day, and ~~writeing~~ **writing** a novel.
>   e. Milagro will quit her job, enter medical school, and ~~she will~~ **become** a doctor.
>   f. David plans to become a writer, an actor, and ~~direct a movie~~ **a movie director**.

2 and 3

- Allow students sufficient time to review their composition and make adjustments.
- You may want to have students highlight any changes they make.

> *Optional activity*
>
> **Class reunion**
>
> Tell students to imagine that it is 20 years in the future and that the class is going to have a reunion. Teach students some expressions such as:
>
> *I haven't seen you for so long!*
> *How have you been?*
> *Look at you – you haven't changed a bit!*
> *You look so different – I didn't recognize you!*
> *Tell me what you've been doing!*
>
> Let students mingle for at least 10 minutes. When the students are finished, ask them what they found out about their classmates.

9 Giving feedback page 89

Say: *We're going to work in small groups to review our compositions.* Divide the class into groups of four.

1

- Read the instructions for Step 1 aloud.
- Have students exchange their compositions and complete 1a–b individually.
- You might have students put their composition inside their book and exchange that as well, so that the partner's comments are recorded in the author's book. Another option is to have readers write their comments on the back of the composition.
- Read the instructions for 1c aloud.
- Have students complete 1c with their group.

2

- Read the instructions for Step 2.
- Call on a student to read the example.
- Tell students to write the letter on a separate piece of lined paper, skipping lines.
- You may want to assign this as homework.

3 and 4

- Have students give the letter to the author.
- Give students a few minutes to answer the question in Step 4.

Just for fun page 90

1

- This is an exercise in which all students write one positive sentence about each of their classmates.
- Arrange the students' chairs in a circle. Have them take out a piece of paper and a pen.
- Read the instructions for Step 1 aloud.
- Call on students to read 1a–e aloud.
- Check that all students understand what they are going to do.
- Have students pass the papers around until they receive their own paper back.

2

- Each student will now have a page full of comments about himself or herself. Let students read their papers.
- You may want to ask students why positive feedback is important. This question can serve as a basis for discussion or as a prompt for a short writing assignment.

10 Architect

Overview

In this unit, students design a college dormitory for international students. They then organize a description of their dormitory and write it in a composition.

This unit introduces the expository organizational mode of division, also known as logical division. Students are also trained in the use of articles. They will make an advertising poster for their dormitory in the final optional lesson.

Key points

Make sure the students understand how to use the dormitory floor-plan page in Part 5.

Encourage students to use colored pencils and let them know that the rooms they include do not have to be shaped exactly like those at the bottom of Part 5. Students can use curved walls, can include interior gardens, and can design the dorm as multiple buildings if they wish.

Spend extra time helping students divide the description of their dorm into subtopics, such as features for "daily living," "study," and "recreation."

Make sure students include a copy of the dorm-design floor plan in their composition.

Give them time afterward to look at and discuss other students' designs.

Sections can be skipped. A minimal set of sections might include Parts 4, 5, 6, and 7. You can also save time by assigning some sections as homework.

1 Brainstorming page 91

Write the headings *Buildings*, *Rooms*, and *Equipment* on the board in three columns.

1

- Read the question and instructions for Step 1 aloud.
- Have students brainstorm individually for five to ten minutes to complete the three lists. You may want to do the brainstorming activity as a class.
- Elicit examples from individual students and write them on the board.

2

- Read the instructions for Step 2 aloud.
- Call on a student to read the examples.
- Give students a few minutes to divide their ideas into smaller groups.
- Say: *There may be some overlap in the function of particular rooms. For example, many people like to study in their dorm room and in the library, or even in the cafeteria.*

3

- Read the instructions for Step 3 aloud.
- Have students compare lists with a partner.
- Go over similarities and differences as a class.

> Later in this unit . . . Call on a student to read this aloud.

2 Analyzing a paragraph page 92

This paragraph uses the development-by-division expository mode. A complex topic is broken down into parts to make it easier to explain. Students will use this mode when they write their own composition.

1

- Read the instructions for Step 1 aloud.
- Have students read the paragraph on their own and complete 1a–d when done.
- Explain the grammar rule behind 1d. When a two-word participial phrase is used as a modifier before a noun, a hyphen is added. When it is used by itself, no hyphen is added.

> **Answers**
> 1. a. Student dorm rooms are the settings for three aspects of a student's life: daily living, study, and recreation.
>   b. *Subtopics:* daily living, study, recreation
>   c. *Attention-getter examples:* Where can you find <u>an unmade bed</u>, <u>books all over the floor</u>, and <u>empty pizza boxes next to a laptop computer?</u>
>   d. study-related furniture
>   student-designed room
>   fully equipped kitchen
>   energy-saving light

> **Answers will vary. Possible answers:**
> 1. a. music I like, music my parents like, music my teenage sister likes
>   b. team sports, pair sports, individual sports
>   c. people I know, people I like, people I love
>   d. good listeners, good lecturers, good activity makers
>   e. money, time, relationships
>   f. clothes, food, entertainment
>   g. writing tools, paper, books
>   h. classrooms, offices, support facilities

2
- Have students compare answers with a partner.
- Call on students to read the paragraph aloud, sentence by sentence.
- Go over the answers as a class.
- Explain that this is a division paragraph, and that students will be writing paragraphs like this for their own compositions.
- If time permits, ask students to divide other things into parts, such as why they like a particular class, the things they talk about with friends, or how they spend free time.

> **Talk about it.** Read this aloud and have students talk with their partners for about five minutes.

2
- Have students compare answers with a partner. If they generated the subtopics with a partner, have them compare in small groups.
- Go over answers as a class.
- Write some examples on the board.

> **Optional activity**
>
> **Categories game**
> Have each student write a topic and three subtopics on an index card. Divide the class into two teams. Give each team the other team's set of cards. Have students take turns choosing cards and reading the subtopics – but not the topics – to their team. If the team guesses the topic correctly, it gets a point.

3 Learning about organization page 93

Read the information box *Division paragraphs* at the top of page 93.

1
- Read the instructions for Step 1 aloud.
- Have students complete 1a–h individually.
- Walk around the classroom and help students as necessary.
- You may want to have students work with a partner to generate the subtopics.

4 Working on content page 94

1
- Read the instructions and question for Step 1 aloud.
- Call on a student to read the e-mail aloud.

2
- Read the instructions and question for Step 2 aloud.
- Call on students to read the list of items. Explain vocabulary as needed.
- Have students work individually to categorize the items. Say: *There may be some overlap in your choices.*

Answers will vary. Possible answers:

2. *Spaces for daily living:*
   cafeteria
   laundry room
   showers
   kitchen
   gym
   Study-related spaces:
   computer room
   copy center
   library
   Recreational spaces:
   game room
   basketball courts
   garden
   sauna
   student lounge
   pond
   pool

3

- Read the instructions for Step 3 aloud.
- Have students choose their favorite items with a partner.
- Ask: *What items would you most like to have in your dormitory?*
- Write several examples on the board.

Optional activity

List expansion

Have students expand the lists from Part 4. Encourage them to be creative. Have them look at the sample poster on page 100 for ideas to add to their lists, such as *indoor greenhouse*, *snack bar*, *rainwater showers*, *a running trail*, and so on.

---

5 Working more on content page 95

You may want to have students complete Part 5 as homework in preparation for the composition they will write in Part 7.

1

- Read the instructions for Step 1 aloud.
- Remind students of the guidelines in the e-mail from Part 4.

2

- Read the instructions for Step 2 aloud.
- Remind students to look at the sample floor plan in Step 1 for reference.
- Give students the option of naming the rooms rather than drawing the icons.
- Encourage them to use more than one color in their design.
- Also tell them to have fun and be creative! For example, the walls may be curved, the dorm may have multiple buildings, and there may be interior gardens as well.

6 Analyzing a model page 96

1

- Read the instructions for Step 1 aloud.
- Have students read the composition individually.
- Call on students to read the composition aloud, paragraph by paragraph.
- Ask: *Which place in the dorm would you most like to visit?*
- Read the instructions for 1a–b aloud and have students follow the directions.

Answers

1. a. *Attention getter:* Live Green!
      Main idea: This dorm has been specially designed for students who enjoy living in nature-filled places.
      Guide: We've included our Live Green theme in facilities for daily living, study, and recreation.
   b. *Paragraph 2:* daily living needs
      Paragraph 3: studying
      Paragraph 4: recreation

2
- Have students compare answers with a partner.
- Go over answers as a class.

7 Write! page 97

1
- Read the instructions for Step 1 aloud.
- Have students complete 1a–c individually.
- If necessary, give students examples of catchy titles.

2
- Read the instructions for Step 2 aloud.
- Have students write their composition on a separate piece of lined paper. Tell them to skip lines so that there will be room for comments and revisions.
- You may want to assign the composition as homework.
- Tell students to include the dorm plan picture at the top of their paper.

3
- Call on a student to read the *Writing checklist* aloud.
- Remind students to check their composition against this list before they turn it in.

8 Editing page 98

Read the information box *Articles* at the top of page 98.

1
- Have students work individually or with a partner to fill in the articles.
- Walk around the classroom, helping students as necessary.
- Go over answers as a class.

> *Answers*
> 1. Let me tell you about **a** college dormitory in Los Angeles. It's at ULA – the University of Los Angeles. Since ULA is **a** big university, **the** dorms are large and have many students living in them. Most of **the** students at ULA are from California, but some of **the** students are from abroad. The dormitory has many suites, which are like small apartments. **The** suites include four bedrooms with two beds each, **a** kitchen, and **a** bathroom. **The** kitchen is large enough for students to cook **a** big meal. **The** dorm students really appreciate this because sometimes **the** cafeteria food is not so good, and they like preparing their own meals. **The** bathroom is also large and has **a** Japanese-style bathtub as well as a Western shower. In addition to **the** suites, there are living rooms on each floor. Each living room has **a** big sofa, some soft chairs, and **a** large-screen television. Everyone says that living in a dorm at ULA is **a** wonderful experience.

2 and 3
- Read the instructions for Steps 2 and 3 aloud.
- Allow students several minutes to review their composition and make any revisions.
- You may want to have students highlight any changes they make.

> *Optional activity*
>
> **More articles practice**
>
> Find a paragraph at your students' reading level that contains numerous articles. Retype the paragraph, omitting the words *a*, *an*, and *the*. Have students fill in the missing articles. Review the activity as a class.

9 Giving feedback page 99

1
- Read the instructions for Step 1 aloud.
- Divide the class into groups of four.
- Have students exchange their compositions with students from another group, then complete 1a–d individually.

50   Unit 10 *Architect*

- You might have students put their composition inside their book and exchange that as well so that the partner's comments are recorded in the author's book. Another option is to have readers write their comments on the back of the composition.

2
- Read the instructions for Step 2 aloud.
- Have students write their letter in the book or on the back of the composition they read.

3
- Read the instructions for Step 3 aloud.
- Have students spend five to ten minutes discussing the compositions and awarding the ribbon. Say: *Be prepared to explain why you chose the design for the award.*
- Discuss the exercise as a class.
- Call on groups to present their favorite designs.

4
- Read the instructions for Step 4 aloud.
- After students receive their compositions back, allow them time to revise as desired.

Just for fun page 100

Tell students that this is an activity in which they can combine their writing and artistic skills to make a poster for their dorm.

1
- Read the instructions for Step 1 aloud.
- Call on students to read the advertisement. Point out the features of the advertisement, such as an advertising slogan, a brief description, contact information, and so on.
- Have students complete their posters individually, in class or at home.
- You may want to have students work in pairs.

2
- Read the instructions for Step 2 aloud.
- Collect the posters and display them around the classroom.
- Have students walk around the classroom to look at the posters. Elicit reactions.

11 My role models

Overview

In this unit, students are asked first to discuss important people in their lives and then to write a composition about one of those people. The composition includes a description of an experience the student had with this person and an explanation of how the experience influenced the student's life.

This unit gives students practice in rearranging the paragraphs of their composition to create different effects. The unit also introduces techniques for good paragraph transition and provides exercises on subject-verb agreement. Students will be given the opportunity to write a letter to their important person in the final optional section.

Key points

Rather than presenting an expository writing mode, this unit concentrates on how ideas are sequenced in the overall composition.

Make sure students understand that being able to come up with a specific incident to write about is a key factor in deciding which person will be their subject.

Maintain a positive classroom environment to encourage openness and self-disclosure.

Sections can be skipped. A minimal set of sections might include Parts 3, 5, 6, and 7. You can also save time by assigning some sections as homework.

1 Brainstorming page 101

1

- Read the questions and instructions for Step 1 aloud.
- Have students brainstorm individually for five to ten minutes to complete their list.
- Remind students that the people on their list should include both people they know personally and famous/important people they have never met.
- Walk around the classroom to encourage and help students as necessary.
- Elicit examples from individual students, and write them on the board.

2

- Divide the class into pairs.
- Read the instructions for Step 2 aloud.
- Ask students to explain to their partner why those people influenced them.
- Remind students to give specific reasons and examples.

> Later in this unit . . . Call on a student to read this aloud.

2 Analyzing paragraphs page 102

These short paragraphs use a variety of expository modes: development by example, definition, division, and so on. The purpose, however, is to show how paragraphs can be linked together in extended prose. Students will use paragraph transition techniques when they write their own composition.

1

- Read the instructions for Step 1 aloud.
- Have students read the composition on their own and complete 1a–d when done.

> **Answers**
> 1. a. Two can be better than one! I have two best friends. Although they are much younger than me, we get along just fine. We eat, read, and **play** together every day.
> We like **games**. Our favorite **game** is "dress up." We put on makeup and costumes in order to look like pirates, princesses, or police officers. Then we laugh and make funny faces. We can spend hours pretending we're other people.
> b. pretending we're other people
> c. do (it) together
> d. In conclusion

2

- Divide the class into pairs and have students compare answers with a partner.
- Call on students to read the composition aloud, paragraph by paragraph.
- Go over answers as a class.
- Explain that these paragraphs are linked together, and that students will be doing this in their own compositions.

> **Talk about it.** Read this aloud and have students talk with their partners for about five minutes.

3 Working on content page 103

1

- Read the instructions for Step 1 aloud.
- Tell students that in making the choice, they should focus on having a good incident to write about rather than just choosing someone they like.
- Tell students that the person does not have to be a close friend or relative.
- Give students a couple of examples of your own role models and the incidents that made you admire these people.
- Give students a few minutes to review their notes from Part 1 and fill in the information.
- Walk around the classroom to encourage and help students as necessary.

2

- Read the instructions for Step 2 aloud.
- Have students tell their partner about the person, relationship, and incident.
- You might call on students to share some of their people and incidents with the class, but you might decide to limit the amount of detail they give so that their stories will still be interesting later, when presented in compositions.

3

- Read the instructions for Step 3 aloud.
- Have students fill in the Subtopic 1 box with additional information about the incident they chose.

4

- Read the instructions for Step 4 aloud.
- Call on students to read the list of subtopics. Elicit "your idea" subtopics from the class as well.
- Have students fill in the remaining two subtopic boxes.

4 Learning about organization
page 104

Read the information box *Development by example* at the top of page 104. An explanation of this expository style can be found at the start of Part 2, *Analyzing paragraphs*.

1

- Read the instructions for Step 1 aloud.
- Call on students to read the two sample arrangements aloud, section by section.
- Ask the class which arrangement they prefer.
- Remind them that there is no one correct answer.

2

- Read the instructions and questions for Step 2 aloud.
- Have students work individually on the arrangement of their composition by filling in the three possibilities in the boxes.
- Walk around the classroom, helping students as necessary.
- Have students discuss their arrangements with a partner.
- Ask students to decide which arrangement they like best.

> **Optional activity**
>
> **Storytelling**
>
> Have students tell their story to a partner in the arrangement they chose. Have them then change partners and tell the story again. This will help them refine the content.

5 Learning more about organization
page 105

Read the information box *Linking paragraphs* at the top of page 105. Explain as necessary.

1
- Read the instructions for Step 1 aloud.
- Have students complete 1a–d individually.
- Go over answers as a class.

> **Answers**
> 1. a. transition words
>   b. repeating an idea
>   c. same words (my mother)
>   d. repeating an idea

2
- Read the instructions for Step 2 aloud.
- Have students complete the step and then share their sentences with a partner.
- Have the partner figure out what kind of link it is.
- Share a few examples as a class.

6 Analyzing a model page 106

1
- Read the instructions for Step 1 aloud.
- Have students read the composition individually.
- Call on students to read the composition aloud, paragraph by paragraph.
- Take a little time to discuss this composition as a class.
- Ask students if they agree that we all must give things up throughout life.
- Call on individual students to express their opinions or share relevant experiences with the class.
- Read the instructions for 1a–c aloud and have students follow the directions.

> **Answers**
> 1. a. From my father, I learned how to accept life as it is.
>   b. Paragraph 2: his father's situation
>   Paragraph 3: incident
>   Paragraph 4: the lesson learned
>   Paragraph 5: conclusion
>   c. *Paragraphs 1 to 2:* repeating an idea (strong and then weak father)
>   "... when he was strong and healthy, but rather when he was weak and ill."
>   +
>   "In fact, my father was once a strong man who loved being active, but a terrible illness took all that away from him."
>   *Paragraphs 2 to 3:* repeating an idea (quiet man)
>   "... he must sit quietly in a chair all day. Even talking is difficult."
>   +
>   "that quiet man"
>   *Paragraphs 3 to 4:* repeating an idea (his words and his thoughtfulness)
>   "... the power to say those words; even in your pain, you think of others first."
>   +
>   "... his thoughtfulness, his words of acceptance."
>   *Paragraphs 4 to 5:* same word (learned)
>   learned
>   +
>   learned

2
- Have students compare answers with a partner.
- Go over answers as a class.

7 Write! page 107

1
- Read the instructions for Step 1 aloud.
- Have students complete the step individually.

2

- Read the instructions for Step 2 aloud.
- Have students read each other's introductory paragraph and comment on whether the three required parts are present.

3

- Read the instructions for Step 3 aloud.
- Have students write their composition on a separate piece of lined paper. Tell them to skip lines so that there will be room for comments and revisions.
- You may want to assign the composition as homework.

4

- Call on a student to read the *Writing checklist* aloud.
- Remind students to check their composition against this list before they turn it in.

Optional activity

Show and tell

Have students bring in pictures of the person they wrote about and give a short presentation to their group. Tell them they should not read from their composition but should speak as naturally as they can. Encourage group members to ask questions.

---

8 Editing   page 108

Read the information box *Subject-verb agreement* at the top of page 108.

1

- Read the instructions for Step 1 aloud.
- Have students work individually or with a partner to complete the step.
- Walk around the classroom, helping students as necessary.
- Go over the answers as a class.

Answers

1. a. likes
   b. has
   c. was
   d. OK
   e. OK
   f. is
   g. OK
   h. OK
   i. was
   j. OK
   k. are
   l. OK

2 and 3

- Read the instructions for Steps 2 and 3 aloud.
- If you want to focus on revising in this course, make any additional suggestions at this time.
- Have students revise their composition.
- You may want to have students highlight any changes they make.

9 Giving feedback   page 109

1

- Have students work in groups of four.
- Read the instructions for Step 1.
- Have each group exchange their four compositions with another group.
- You might have students put their composition inside their book and exchange that as well, so that the partner's comments are recorded in the author's book. Another option is to have readers write their comments on the back of the composition.

2 and 3

- Read the instructions for Steps 2 and 3 aloud.
- Have students circle the expression that best describes the composition they just read. Then tell them to go on to Step 3.
- Walk around the classroom to encourage and help students as necessary.
- You may want to have students exchange the composition they just read within their group, after they finish working on Step 3.

4

- Have students write their note or e-mail.
- You may choose to have students write their note on a separate piece of lined paper (or, as suggested above, in the author's book or on the back of the composition). That way, they can then give both the composition and letter back to the author.

5 and 6

- Read the instructions for Steps 5 and 6 aloud.
- Have the students give their note to the author.
- Ask them to discuss or write down things they could do to make their composition better.
- Share a few of the ideas with the class.

> **Optional activity**
> **More agreement practice**
> Have students write sentences about students in the class using *each*, *every*, *neither*, *one of*, *someone*, *anything*, *everywhere*, and *nobody*.

Just for fun page 110

1 and 2

- This is an enjoyable exercise that you may want students to complete on their own.
- Read the instructions for Step 1 aloud.
- Call on students to read the example letter, paragraph by paragraph.
- Have students write their letter.

3

- Read the instructions for Step 3 aloud.
- Give students the option of sending their letters.
- You can invite students to share their letter with their classmates, but students may want to keep their letter private.

12 Be a reporter

Overview

This final unit is a special project to finish the course. Students study newspaper writing and write articles on local events. The articles are then collected, put into a newspaper or magazine format, and copied as a class newspaper for other students to read.

This unit teaches students to use objective, persuasive, and entertaining writing styles for different types of newspaper articles. Students also learn how to write headlines and use a variety of verbs instead of just repeating the same one, such as "said," over and over again. In the final *Just for fun* section, the students put all their articles together and apply some basic principles of graphic design in order to make a class newspaper.

Key points

The class newspaper is an end-of-the-course culminating activity.

Emphasize that different newspaper articles use different styles of writing and try to answer five *Wh-* questions: *who*, *what*, *when*, *where*, and *why*.

To produce a publication that really looks like a newspaper, assess the students' computer skills beforehand and make reservations in a computer lab. If a computer is not available, have students type the articles and then "cut and paste" them to make a newspaper.

Consider different ways to distribute the final product.

This unit may take more class time than the others, but sections can be skipped. A minimal set of sections might include Parts 3, 4, 6, and 7. You can also save time by assigning some sections as homework.

1 Brainstorming page 111

1 and 2

- Read the instructions for Step 1 aloud.
- Have a student read the examples in the list, and then have students brainstorm individually for five to ten minutes to complete their list.
- Have students compare their list with a partner and mark the most interesting topics.

3

- Read the instructions for Step 3 aloud.
- Elicit topics from the class and write them on the board.
- Encourage a variety of topics, including topics about the school and community.

4

- Read the instructions for Step 4 aloud.
- Have students write in their book the three topics that most interest them.
- You may want to monitor students' topic choices to get a balanced set of articles for the newspaper.

> Later in this unit . . . Call on a student to read this aloud.

2 Analyzing paragraphs page 112

These paragraphs use a variety of expository modes: development by example, process, and so on. The purpose, however, is to show how different writing styles are used when the purposes of the articles are different. Students will use a variety of writing styles when they write their own compositions.

1

- Read the instructions for Step 1 aloud.
- Call on students to read the three articles, and then have them complete 1a–d.

> **Answers**
>
> 1. a. A – Front page news
>   B – Society section
>   C – Editorials
>   b. *Fact in Article A:* George DeBartolo, a popular teacher at Markson High School, has decided to retire this year after 20 years of teaching tenth- and eleventh-grade English.
>   c. *Who?* George DeBartolo
>   *What?* retirement party
>   *When?* last night
>   *Where?* La Maison Restaurant
>   *Why?* he is retiring/to honor this great teacher
>   d. *Opinion in article C:* one of our best teachers

2

- Divide the class into pairs and have the students compare answers with a partner.
- Call on students to read each article aloud.
- Go over answers as a class.
- Discuss as a class which article is most interesting. Ask individual students to explain why.
- Explain that these articles use different styles of writing and that students will be using these styles in their own compositions.
- You may want to elicit additional examples of other newspaper pages or sections. If possible, bring an English-language newspaper to class and have students look at it.

> **Talk about it.** Read this aloud and have students talk with their partners for about five minutes.

> **Optional activity**
>
> **Comparing and contrasting newspapers**
>
> Bring in or ask your students to bring in different kinds of newspapers. Have students work in groups to compare them. Ask students to find differences or similarities in layout, typeface, pictures, and content. You can find many newspapers on the Internet.

3 Learning about organization
page 113

Read the information box *Using objective, persuasive, and entertaining styles* at the top of page 113.

1

- Read the instructions for Step 1 aloud.
- Tell the students that they can make up any information they'd like for their articles.
- Tell them to write articles for each picture, using the style indicated.
- Each article should be two or three sentences in length if written in the book, but you can ask for longer articles if students write them on separate pieces of lined paper.
- Since this activity requires a fair amount of time, you might assign it as homework.

2

- Put students in pairs or groups to read each other's articles and offer comments.
- If using groups, you might have them read all the group's articles and have students star one or two they like.
- Share a few of the better, or more interesting, articles with the class.

4 Working on content page 114

1

- Read the instructions for Step 1 aloud.
- Ask students if they know all the listed article types and explain as necessary.
- Rather than letting students decide on the types of articles they would like to write, you might assign them to individuals or groups in order to get a good balance of article types.

2

- Read the instructions for Step 2 aloud.
- Have students work individually to list three topics and styles.

58 Unit 12 *Be a reporter*

3

- Read the instructions for Step 3 aloud.
- Write some of the topics from Step 2 on the board, and have students as a class vote on the articles they would like to include.
- Decide who will write each article.
- Finally, work out which articles go together in what sections of the newspaper, and what order the sections will occur.
- If necessary, you might set article word length limits.

5 Learning more about organization
page 115

Read the information box *Newspaper headlines and styles* at the top of page 115.

1

- Read the instructions for Step 1 aloud.
- Have the students complete 1a–f on their own.
- Have students compare answers with a partner.
- Go over answers as a class.
- At this point, explain that headlines are written in a way to make the topic clear, to attract readers, and to use as few words as possible. The latter is why they use a reduced form, such as leaving out articles (*a*, *an*, and *the*).

> **Answers**
> 1. a. editorial/persuasive
>   b. news report/objective
>   c. review/entertaining
>   d. fashion/entertaining
>   e. news report/objective
>   f. how-to suggestions/persuasive

2

- Read the instructions for Step 2 aloud.
- Have students work individually to write headlines.
- Also have students write a headline for the article they were assigned in Part 4, if it is not among the three article topics that students wrote in the Part 4 chart.

3

- Divide the class into pairs.
- Read the instructions for Step 3 aloud.
- Have students read their headlines to their partner, who will guess what kind of article type each headline is for.
- Remind students that they can find article types at the top of page 114.
- Share a few of the more interesting headlines as a class. Write them on the board and ask students what kinds of articles they are for.

> *Optional activity*
> **What's the headline?**
> Bring in copies of four to six short newspaper articles with the headlines removed. Put students into groups to write an appropriate headline for each article. Compare ideas as a class before supplying the actual headlines.

6 Analyzing a model page 116

1

- Read the instructions for Step 1 aloud.
- Have students read the composition individually.
- Call on students to read the composition aloud, paragraph by paragraph.
- Read the instructions for 1a–c aloud and have students follow the directions.

> **Answers**
> 1. a. entertaining
>   b. *Who?* Cindy Certello
>   *What?* returned home
>   *When?* recently, after spending two years away
>   *Where?* North Brookfield, MA
>   *Why?* to get married and teach Spanish
>   c. 5: fiancé's comments
>   2: changes
>   4: mother's comments
>   3: future plans

Unit 12 *Be a reporter* 59

2

- Have students compare answers with a partner.
- Go over answers as a class.

7 Write! page 117

- Before starting, think about what kind of newspaper you would like the class to make and what kinds of articles you want in it.
- Make a plan to assign the type of article each student should write, or list the article topics they choose on the board and either approve those choices or direct them to other topics. That way, you can ensure the newspaper will have a variety of topics and balance between article types.

1

- Read the instructions for Step 1 aloud.
- Have students brainstorm articles individually.
- Give each student a different article to write.

2 and 3

- Read the instructions for Steps 2 and 3 aloud.
- Have students complete the steps individually.
- Go over answers as a class and offer additional input as necessary.

4

- Read the instructions for Step 4 aloud.
- Have students write their article on a separate piece of lined paper. Tell them to skip lines so that there will be room for comments and revisions.
- You may want to assign the article writing as homework.

5

- Call on a student to read the *Writing checklist* aloud.
- Remind students to check their article against this list before they turn it in.

8 Editing page 118

Read the information box *Verb variety* at the top of page 118.

1

- Read the instructions for Step 1 aloud.
- Give students time to look at the model and write down their answers, individually or in pairs.
- Walk around the classroom, helping students as necessary.
- Go over the answers as a class.

Answer
1. exclaimed, commented, stated, remarked

2

- Read the instructions for Step 2 aloud.
- Read the list of words and comment on the nuances of these terms.
- Give the students a few minutes to add more words, and then compare them as a class.
- Write some answers on the board and ask students to add any additional words to their list.

3

- Read the instructions for Step 3 aloud.
- Point out a couple of cases where words do not fit, such as *ask* in the first blank.
- Have students complete the step individually and then either compare answers with a partner or share them with the class.

> *Answers may vary. Possible answers:*
>
> 3. Residents of Canton, Ohio, were surprised yesterday to find that City Hall had been painted yellow during the night. Mayor Joan Carter **explained**, "We don't know who did it or how it happened. We are looking for the mysterious painter now. But," she **admitted**, laughing, "it's a nice color. I like it better than gray."
>   Not all of the town residents agree. Gavin Wang, a dentist, **complained**, "I think it's terrible. Whoever did this should be punished."
>   "Who did such a thing?" **asked** Barbara Koh, a grocery store owner. "No building is safe anymore," she **claimed**. "Where were the police?" she **demanded**.
>   Police officer Mark Morris **responded**, "We don't have any clues, but we're doing our best." He **stated** that he had a detective working on the case.
>   Hadas Bori, 6 years old, was very happy to see the brightly colored building on her way to school. "It's pretty!" she **shouted**. "I want someone to paint my school building the same color," she **exclaimed**.

4 and 5

- Read the instructions for Steps 4 and 5 aloud.
- If you want to focus on revising in this course, make any additional suggestions at this time.
- Have students revise their composition.
- You may want to have students highlight any changes they make.

> *Optional activity*
>
> **More word variety**
>
> Do the same activity with other common verbs such as *go*, *look*, or *hit*. You might try this with adjectives as well, such as *good* or *happy*.

9 Giving feedback page 119

1

- Divide the class into groups. If possible, choose each group's members according to the type of article they wrote.
- Read the instructions for Step 1 aloud.
- Have students exchange articles within their groups and complete 1a–b individually.
- You might have students put their composition in their book and exchange that as well so that the partner's comments are recorded in the author's book. Another option is to have readers write their comments on the back of the composition.

2 and 3

- Read the instructions for Steps 2 and 3 aloud.
- Once students finish reading all the articles and choose one they agree on as being their favorite, have them draw a ribbon, draw a star, or write the words "Pulitzer Prize winner" on it.
- If you do the *Just for fun* activity, making a class newspaper, you won't have to announce the winners, but if not, do so.

4

- Read the instructions for Step 4 aloud.
- Ask the students to look over the suggestions, make revisions if needed, and then submit the final articles to you for the class newspaper after doing the *Just for fun* activity.

Just for fun page 120

- This group activity is an excellent way for students to learn about graphic design, computers, and journalism. It also gives you and your students a keepsake from the class.
- Divide students into groups according to areas of responsibility for the newspaper. One group can be responsible for proofreading or editing, another for typing, another for layout, another for artwork, another for type design and/or photos, and so on.

1

- Read the instructions for Step 1 aloud.
- Discuss the design of the model newspaper.

2

- Read the instructions for Step 2 aloud.
- Explain that serif fonts are typefaces that have little hooks on them (e.g., Times and Courier). Sans serif fonts (e.g., Geneva and Helvetica) do not have hooks.
- Have students study the model layout.
- You may want to bring in an actual newspaper to examine as well.

- Have students work as a class to come up with a basic design, including grid, the typefaces they will use, and so on.
- Make sure everyone writes down this information.

3 and 4

- Read the instructions for Steps 3 and 4 aloud.
- Have some students work on word-processed versions of their articles while groups work on the sections. Make sure the design is consistent throughout.
- Assemble the final newspaper, make copies, and distribute.
- Allow enough time for this project. It may take several class sessions as well as outside work to complete.

Typing tips. Read this aloud and answer any questions that students may have.

Optional activities

Getting feedback

After students finish their newspaper, have them make copies and distribute it to other groups or classes. Have them insert a reader survey form in the copies, with questions such as *What did you like about our newspaper? Which article did you find the most interesting?* and *Can you suggest any improvements?* The surveys should include a way for readers to return them.

Write us!

Encourage students to write to us, the authors. We would also enjoy hearing your feedback. Send letters to:

Arlen Gargagliano and Curtis Kelly
Cambridge University Press
32 Avenue of the Americas
New York, NY 10013

CPSIA information can be obtained at www.ICGtesting.com
Printed in the USA
LVOW02s2312070115

421766LV00002B/19/P